The Tragic Idea

CLASSICAL INTER/FACES

Series editors: Susanna Braund and Paul Cartledge

Also in the series:

**The Delusions of Invulnerability: Wisdom and Morality
in Ancient Greece, China and Today**
G.E.R. Lloyd

Gender and the Interpretation of Classical Myth
Lillian E. Doherty

Lucretius and the Modern World
W.R. Johnson

Pity Transformed
David Konstan

Plato's Progeny
Melissa Lane

Radical Theatre
Rush Rehm

Translating Words, Translating Cultures
Lorna Hardwick

THE TRAGIC IDEA

Vassilis Lambropoulos

Duckworth

First published in 2006 by
Gerald Duckworth & Co. Ltd.
90-93 Cowcross Street, London EC1M 6BF
Tel: 020 7490 7300
Fax: 020 7490 0080
inquiries@duckworth-publishers.co.uk
www.ducknet.co.uk

A catalogue record for this book is available
from the British Library

ISBN 0 7156 3558 1
EAN 9780715635582

Typeset by e-type, Liverpool
Printed and bound in Great Britain by
CPI Bath

Contents

Contents

Introduction

This book traces the origins of the 'tragic', the modern idea that there exists a distinct quality that can be identified as tragic. Since the 1790s, this quality has been attributed to every domain, feature and function known to humankind, from life to cosmos, and from culture to society. The term has entered the vocabulary of existence and experience, description and evaluation, high reflection and common argument. It has been broadly present in major systems of thought, art and scholarship during the nineteenth and twentieth centuries. Starting with the Romantics, thinkers and artists have been engaging with the genre of tragedy as both a repertoire of past achievement and a responsibility of future art, while also exploring a dark dimension of life which they call tragic sense, experience, vision, paradox, fate or spirit. Literary Romanticism in the 1790s, philosophical existentialism in the 1920s and political radicalism in the 1960s are three movements driven by particularly forceful tragic views; but interest in the tragic is so common that it has even been attributed to writers who did not embrace it in any explicit way, such as Karl Marx, Simone Weil, Hannah Arendt, Theodor Adorno and Michel Foucault. In general, it is quite fair to claim that a certain tragic feeling permeates modern thought:

> The major philosophical systems since the French Revolution have been tragic systems. ... The metaphors are various: the Fichtean and Hegelian concepts of self-alienation, the Marxist scenario of economic servitude, Schopenhauer's diagnosis of human conduct as harnessed to coercive will, the Nietzschean analysis of decadence, Freud's narrative of the coming of neurosis and discontent after the original Oedipal crime, the Heideggerian ontology of a fall from the primal truth of Being. To philosophize after Rousseau and Kant, to find a normative, conceptual phrasing of the psychic, social, and historical condi-

7

tion of man, is to think 'tragically'. It is to find in tragic drama ... the 'opus metaphysicum par excellence'.

Steiner 1984: 2

The currency of the idea of the tragic has made it difficult to remember how modern this usage is. Indeed, before the early German Romantics the tragic pertained to tragic drama alone: from Aristotle to Lessing, tragic figures, events or lessons were recognized only on the stage, and were meaningful within this particular dramatic genre alone. No theorist from Hellenistic Greece, Renaissance Italy, Baroque Spain, Neo-classical France or Enlightenment England would have used the term in a literal sense outside the theatre. The tragic is abstracted from drama and its circumstances for the first time at a fascinating moment in history when moral, political and artistic demands converge in the German confrontation with modernity. A complex quest for justice, freedom and beauty creates the new ancients, the Greeks – the ancients of modernity. The tragic idea represents an integral part of the modern Greek project as it is first formulated in Germany and gradually spreads around the world. Since the French Revolution made palpable the ethical tensions of modern freedom, the tragic has come to represent the difficulties of resolution. What can account for this impressive trajectory? What exactly is the import of the term that makes it deeply meaningful to so many directions of feeling and inquiry?

Following a few introductory reminders of pre-Romantic dramatic theory, this book traces the first century and a half of the tragic, from Schiller to Heidegger, while in the epilogue it glances at its fate since the 1930s and speculates on its future. It does not consider classical drama (Cartledge 1997, Rehm 2003) or the theory of tragedy, ancient (Halliwell 1998) and modern (Carlson 1993), and as a result it does not discuss the Romans (Erasmo 2004), since the abstract tragic quality has been always derived from the Greeks. Neither does it consider the presence of ancient drama on the modern stage in terms of revival, adaptation or influence (Patsalidis and Sakellaridou 1999, McDonald and Walton 2002, Wetmore Jr 2002, Hall et al. 2004). It limits itself almost exclusively to writers who named and discussed the tragic as such.

Introduction

This project owes much to Peter Szondi's landmark *An Essay on the Tragic* (2002 [originally 1961]), and it gladly acknowledges its debt by adopting that book's ingenious structure. At the same time, it diverges from it in crucial respects, such as the breadth of geographical and chronological coverage. In his book, which stands as an unacknowledged memorial to the exhausted German tradition, Szondi attempts an explanation of the notion's history:

> The history of the philosophy of the tragic is itself not free from the tragic. It resembles the flight of Icarus. The closer thought comes to the general concept, the less that the substantial, the source of thought's uplift, adheres to it. Reaching the height of insight into the structure of the tragic, thought collapses, powerless. At the point where a philosophy, as a philosophy of the tragic, becomes more than the knowledge of the dialectic around which its fundamental concepts assemble, at the point where such a philosophy no longer determines its own tragic outcome, it is no longer philosophy. It therefore appears that philosophy cannot grasp the tragic – or that there is no such thing as *the* tragic.
>
> Szondi 2002: 49

Like Szondi's book, however, this account is itself a tragic one, that is, an account based on the tragedy of dialectics. We are left wondering whether the tragic is beyond our grasp or perhaps has never existed. A more adequate explanation ought to be less in thrall to the material it analyses. In this regard, recent volumes (Burke 2003, Grass 1999, Wellbery 2004) with a similar episodic structure have provided excellent correctives. While Szondi composed an explicitly Hegelian essay which saw itself as part of the specifically German elaboration of the idea, this volume offers a genealogy of the concept that incorporates philosophical as well as cultural parameters of its evolution. As a historicist genealogy, it aims to provide sufficient intellectual context (in terms of issues, discourses and trends) for readers to follow the main debates on the tragic. However, adding a broader socio-historical framework or discussion of more writers would have violated the page limit of the Classical Inter/Faces series.

The volume does not demand to be read sequentially. Although it does tell a story, it eschews organic development in favour of formation, namely, the ongoing reconfiguration of a supreme 'truth', the tragic essence. The genealogy focuses microscopically on representative articulations of the notion, which take the form of aphoristic quotations by successive writers. Such quotations make possible an examination of the tragic in resonant configurations, sometimes moving vertically into other works of the same thinker or laterally into works by other authors. One author does not necessarily lead to the next. Sometimes a thread is dropped and picked up later. Even though the model is not a genetic one of the transmission of ideas (one author's position directly engendering another's), the remarkable density of time (a century and a half), place (Europe) and gender (male) bring to the surface an interesting sociological dimension of the circulation of this concept: namely, that most of those interested in the tragic had strong personal connections among themselves. They were neighbours, friends, fellow students, colleagues, interlocutors, collaborators and the like. Thus the book maps a philosophical conversation that crossed geographical, linguistic, ideological, religious and other borders in order to bring major thinkers together (metaphorically but often also literally) as participants in a common inquiry into the tragic contradictions of liberty.

Initially, within the framework of the antinomies of modern liberty, the tragic stands for contradiction within human autonomy, for the conflict of freedom and necessity, liberation and legislation. Later, once dialectics grows more systematic and absorbs contradiction into its very operation, the idea is also identified with what overflows, surpasses, oversteps human horizons – with whatever exceeds reason, knowledge, understanding, history, justice, kinship and so on. The tragic represents what goes beyond but does not and cannot transcend. Thus throughout its unfolding, the tragic has played an ethical role without acquiring a fixed moral value. Within the speculative and the ontologic, it represents 'the place where the system fails to circle back on itself, where the systematic does not quite succeed in its overlay of the historic, where the circularity (as Szondi says) modifies itself and becomes a spiral' (Lacoue-Labarthe 1978: 72) without return or relief. Very often, it has operated as a supplement to aesthetics. The aesthetic reconciles opposite faculties

10

(reason and sensibility, understanding and feeling). Ethical issues that cannot be reconciled or adjudicated by aesthetic arbitration find a haunting expression in the tragic idea.

As first established by Idealism, the tragic signifies constitutive self-division: it announces the necessary split of a primordial unity, the reflective instance of substance, and the emergence of individuation into history. As such, it helps the Moderns come to terms with contingency by relying less on an Enlightenment idea of progress than on the Romantic feeling of destiny. In sum, the tragic idea has opened up the following possibilities:

(a) ethical possibilities in the face of the internal contradictions of history and freedom;
(b) political possibilities in the face of the defeat of the revolution and the ensuing dilemmas of justice;
(c) artistic possibilities in the face of the collapse of Neo-humanist genres and forms and the dissolution of Neo-classical audiences; and
(d) philosophical possibilities in the face of the incompatible demands of liberalism and scepticism which tested the limits of reason.

'Indeed, as the love affair between Athenian tragedy and German Idealism clearly exhibits, the "tragic" is one way of reconciling the aesthetic, the ethical and the political' (Taxidou 2004: 1).

In an effort to keep such possibilities open, the approach of this book is neither essentialist (embracing the tragic as a perennial feature of the world) nor constructivist (rejecting it as an oppressive principle of Eurocentric domination). Rather, it respects the historical specificity of the notion and its ethico-political contributions. Moreover, it does not conclude that the tragic has exhausted its creative potential. Dramatic refunctionings may keep the tragic idea consequential for the coming uncertain times.

In conclusion, a remark of a disciplinary nature for the reader of the splendid series which has honoured this volume by including it in its list. The tragic is an extremely demanding subject for several reasons: for example, it is a very abstract (and not at all practical) issue and it is deeply Germanic too (that is, steeped in the legacy of Idealism). Those who discussed it during the period under examination had a limited, if not idiosyncratic, knowledge of Greek and did not always scrutinize the accuracy of the editions they used. The present author (who works in comparative literature, specializing in post-Byzantine Greek as well as Western Hellenism) has made every effort to quote the most reliable and accessible translation of their work and to analyse it for a general, non-specialized academic readership. Classicists may still find the volume demanding though in the end they may be inspired by the polyphonic conversation on the tragic which continues well into the third millennium. Whether they are interested in the classical tradition or not, they may deem the adventures of this uniquely modern view of moral autonomy and responsibility worthy of renewed attention.

Acknowledgements

Personal and professional circumstances delayed the completion of this manuscript by four years. The author is grateful to the press, and especially to Deborah Blake, for their understanding and support. In addition to trust, Susanna Braund and Paul Cartledge, the editors of the series, offered inestimable guidance and advice. Paul, in particular, commented in eye-opening detail on two successive versions of the entire work. Margaret Haynes was a meticulous and highly sophisticated copyeditor. John Chioles, Gregory Jusdanis, Artemis Leontis, Peter Murphy, Timothy Reiss and Vivasvan Soni also enriched the manuscript with their suggestions and corrections. Beau Case provided valuable bibliographic guidance. Erin Mays, Chris Apostoleris and Peter Hasiakos, while undergraduate students at the University of Michigan, contributed superb research assistance. The author is happy to have worked with all the above and to acknowledge his great debt to each one of them. He dedicates this book to his parents, Polymnia Loumpouridis and Dionysios Lambropoulos.

Charles de Marguetel de Saint-Évremond (1672)

René Rapin (1674)

Nowadays, we see men represented upon the theatre without the interposition of the gods, and this conduct is infinitely more useful both to the public and to private persons, for in our tragedies we neither introduce any villain who is not detested nor any hero who does not cause himself to be admired. With us, few crimes escape unpunished and few virtues go off unrewarded. In short, by the good examples we publicly represent on the theatre, by the agreeable sentiments of love and admiration that are discreetly interwoven with a rectified fear and pity, we are in a capacity of arriving to that perfection which Horace [in *The Art of Poetry*] desires – *Omne tulit punctum qui miscuit utile dulci* [he gets every vote who mixes the useful and delightful] – which can never be effected by the rules of the ancient tragedy.

Saint-Évremond, 'On Ancient and Modern Tragedy',
quoted in Dukore 1974: 276

Hence it proceeds that these [contemporary French] tragedies mixed with gallantries never make such admirable impressions on the spirit as did those of Sophocles and Euripides, for all the bowels were moved by the great objects of terror and pity which they proposed. 'Tis likewise for this that the reputation of our modern tragedies so soon decays and yields but small delight at two years' end, whereas the Greeks please yet to those that gave a good taste after two thousand years, because what is not grave and serious in the theatre, though it give delight at present, after a short time grows distasteful and unpleasant, and because what is not proper for great thoughts and great figures in tragedy cannot support itself.

Rapin, *Reflections on Aristotle's Treatise of Poesy*,
quoted in Dukore 1974: 267

From Spain to Poland and from the German to the Greek lands, the first consciously modern writing was the composition of modern tragedy, and it generated a lot of critical reflection on the tasks of imaginative writing. The democratization of criticism and the subsequent formation of the first modern literary culture, including the 'public', took shape in debates about the form and meaning of tragedy, especially under the impact of the momentous recuperation of Greek plays and the harmonization of Aristotle's *Poetics* with Horace's *Ars poetica* (Javitch 1999). Between the fifteenth and the seventeenth century tragedy 'was so fundamental to the establishment of vernaculars, the development of literature, the making of national theatres, to political, religious, educational, and epistemological debate, indeed, to the "passage to modernity", as to make its study central to any understanding of modern Western culture' (Reiss 1999: 229).

For example, in the seventeenth century, French dramatic theory circulates through prefaces, pamphlets, treatises and reports all over Europe, stirring public 'quarrels' among both specialists and the public about specific plays as well as general issues. These publications furnish an early model for critical debate. Near the end of the century, certain critics disagree over the merits of ancient and modern tragedy, balancing their criteria quite differently. Writing in his 'On Ancient and Modern Tragedy' (1672), Saint-Évremond (1610-1703) praises contemporary drama because it combines useful/moral with delightful/agreeable elements, something that the ancient rules did not encourage. René Rapin (1621-87), taking an opposite view in his *Reflections on Aristotle's Treatise of Poesy* (1674), criticizes it for mixing the two Horatian injunctions at the cost of gravity and greatness which have now disappeared. Such disagreements will soon escalate in the heated French Quarrel of the Ancients and the Moderns (1687-1719) and the British Battle of the Books in the 1690s, in which the legitimacy of modernity, and not just the rules and proprieties, was at stake.

> The Battle was proclaimed, defined, and won by the Moderns (who, by the way, assigned to their opponents the position of the Ancients). While their argument took the form of philosophy versus taste in France and that of science versus faith in

England, their greatest success on both fronts was the substitution of art and literature for piety and faith. In the Battle of the Books – the first conscious and open conflict in the west of Old and New, tradition and modernity – the ancient past emerged as past history. Literature and the arts appeared as modern, and intrinsic interpretation was deemed the right approach to them while poetics gradually lost its normative character.

Lambropoulos 1993: 44-5

In this context, the question of tragedy remains important as a theatrical issue and, in addition, begins to acquire broader literary and historical significance.

Jean-François Marmontel (1765)

Man falls into danger and into misfortune through a cause which is *outside him* or *within him*. *Outside him*, it is his destiny, his situation, his duties, his bonds, all the accidents of life, and the action which the gods, nature, and other men exercise on him. ... *Within him*, it is his weakness, his imprudence, his inclinations, his passions, his vices, sometimes his virtues; of these causes, the most fruitful, the most pathetic, and the most moral is passion combined with natural goodness. ... This distinction of the causes of misfortune, either *outside us*, or *within us*, brings about the division into two systems of tragedy, the ancient and the modern.

Marmontel, in the *Encyclopédie*, quoted in Dukore 1974: 290

In the Neo-classical era, the Moderns begin to define themselves in opposition to an irrevocable past and an exhausted tradition. While many writers debate the meaning of formal values and principles of writing, and discussions of tragedy remain closely connected to the theatrical experience (from composition to performance to response), a sense of historical distance emerges in the wake of the Quarrel. Rejecting ancient tragedy in favour of contemporary 'serious dramatic genre', Beaumarchais exclaims in 1767: 'What do the revolutions of Athens and Rome mean to me, the quiet subject of an eighteenth-century monarchy?' (quoted in Dukore 1974: 301). In the entry on 'Tragedy' (1765) in the *Encyclopédie* (1755-80), edited by Denis Diderot, Jean-François Marmontel (1723-99) wonders whether the difference between ancient and modern plays is not just technical but philosophical. What if the two systems are separated not by stylistic divergences but by entire worldviews? If the Ancients were marked by destiny, are they now turning into the destiny of the Moderns? The Moderns may well be those who can no longer feel ancient or be classical.

David Hume (1757)

It seems an unaccountable pleasure, which the spectators of a well-written tragedy receive from sorrow, terror, anxiety, and other passions, that are in themselves disagreeable and uneasy. The more they are touched and affected, the more they are delighted with the spectacle; ... What is it then, which in this case raises a pleasure from the bosom of uneasiness, so to speak; and a pleasure, which still retains all the features and outward symptoms of distress and sorrow? I answer: This extraordinary effect proceeds from that very eloquence, with which the melancholy scene is represented.

Hume, 'Of Tragedy', quoted in Dukore 1974: 421

Written in prose and not elaborate verse, domestic tragedy takes hold early in the eighteenth century and achieves international appeal by presenting the common and everyday, instead of mythical or historical heroism. Dramatic theory too turns to such psychological issues as emotional stimulation, marking the moment when the modern paradox of tragedy emerges: how do spectators convert passions aroused by sorrowful events into an experience of enjoyment? Discussing French Neo-classical views of pleasure and pain, David Hume (1711-76) proposes in his essay 'Of Tragedy' (1757) that the source of pleasure in tragic drama is the artistry of eloquence, the beauty of oratory, the force of expression which generate it. While the events of the play are themselves awful and the passions they arouse disagreeable, the depiction of painful material by the fine arts 'affords the highest entertainment' (422), because painful emotions are transformed by the infusion of the feeling of artistic enjoyment. Artistic qualities balance sorrowful emotions. In the essay, these qualities have not become aesthetic yet. They pertain to feelings and passions of the audience (sadness over devastating occurrences, joy over noble artistry), not features of the work itself. Modifying the view quoted from Fontenelle's famous essay on the Ancients and the

Moderns (1688), Hume reflects on response and studies varieties of psychological experience as he is interested in the overall pleasure which helps 'dismiss the audience with entire satisfaction and contentment' (423).

Gotthold Ephraim Lessing (1768)

To what end the hard work of dramatic form? Why build a theatre, disguise men and women, torture their memories, invite the whole town to assemble at one place if I intend to produce nothing more with my work and its representation, than some of those emotions that would be produced as well by any good story that everyone could read by his chimney-corner at home?

Lessing, *Hamburg Dramaturgy*, quoted in Dukore 1974: 435

Like many Enlightenment intellectuals, Gotthold Ephraim Lessing (1729-81) explores the uses of artistic enjoyment for human improvement, as he is committed to the social responsibility of culture. In the *Letter to M. d'Alembert on the Theatre* (1758), Rousseau declared that theatre cannot function as a moral institution since it exists primarily to amuse. A decade later, Lessing derives a moral function from the pleasure that drama provides, that is, from the very feature that made Rousseau claim that theatre can have no educational effect. He suggests that theatrical pleasure awakens in the audience pity or compassion, a virtue honoured by Rousseau himself and recognized much earlier by Aristotle. Here a reinterpretation of the poetics of catharsis (which Rousseau denied) results in Lessing's theory of moral compassion and promotes an aesthetics of emotional effect. The Renaissance project of normative poetics as organized in Lodovico Castelvetro's commentary *Poetica d'Aristotele vulgarizzata e sposta* (1570) around the authority of reason and the economy of the unities comes to a close. The arts are now to be judged according to their effects on the emotions of the audience rather than any objective rules.

By contrasting the principles of French Neo-classicism with those of Aristotelian poetics, Lessing introduces Germany to the debate between the Ancients and the Moderns. In 1768, he devotes eleven issues of the *Hamburg Dramaturgy* (1767-9) to an extended polemic against Pierre Corneille's tragic theory which, he claims, has been

19

undermined by French tragedy. Exploring the operations of Aristotelian catharsis, Lessing studies pity and fear, and finds that the former has a more constructive impact than French writers thought, a conclusion fitting with the goals of the bourgeois tragedy that he himself is writing and promoting. The successful combination of pity and fear engages the audience emotionally while their purgation provides it with moral schooling.

Lessing conceives of this schooling as national education. What differentiates his attitude from English and French theory (both of which he knows well) is that he sees the stage as part of the national culture that should be judged as 'the school of the moral world' of civil society. The new intelligentsia that emerges after 1750 and writes for the new reading public of the middle class proposes that, until Germany acquires a constitution, the path to national identity is the formation of a collective moral character that will free the people from the yoke of foreign imitation. That should be the mission of a truly German theatre. To serve it, national theatre requires a proper understanding of the origins of drama. Lessing contributes to it by showing again and again how the French (and, by implication, German rationalist dramatic theory) totally misrepresented the Ancients.

As the theatrical public is becoming a bourgeois audience, the constitution and education of the community remain particularly important. By combining the writing of plays in the new dramatic form of domestic tragedy with the practice of dramatic criticism (including reviews of performances) and the study of poetics, the first great German 'man of letters' is hoping to contribute to the creation and edification of a national audience. This is the role that modern tragedy and its theory are called to play. His cultural criticism does not provide absolute moral or artistic standards but rather guidance in public taste for the communal assembly.

For at least another generation, the harmonization of national culture through the moral growth of civic life and aesthetic experience remains a paramount concern. In his first major essay, 'The Stage Considered as a Moral Institution' (1785), Schiller radicalizes positions taken earlier by Diderot and Mercier in France as he surveys all the critical contributions of drama to society and state: the stage assists justice, serves as a companion to wisdom and religion, shames fools by wit and satire, serves as a practical guide through social life, combats errors in education, enlightens opinion about government, cultivates the national spirit, and in general provides both pleasure and instruction (Schiller 1959). Thus drama promotes on the local level what Herder called 'education of humanity', acting like a 'tribunal' (Bloch 1988: 238) and fulfilling its role as a public institution with moral jurisdiction over the political realm. However, the confidence in morality that drama and criticism share is about to be jolted by the new philosophical project of autonomy which will privilege ethical will over civic life.

Immanuel Kant (1785)

What else can freedom of will be but autonomy – that is, the property which will has of being a law to itself? The proposition 'Will is in all its actions a law to itself' expresses, however, only the principle of acting on no maxim other than one which can have for its object itself as at the same time a universal law. This is precisely the formula of the categorical imperative and the principle of morality. Thus a free will and a will under moral law are one and the same.

Kant 1964: 114

The German participation in the revolutionary enthusiasm of the 1780s is unique in its philosophical intensity. 'Philosophy suddenly became the key rallying point for an entire generation of German intellectuals, all of whom had begun reading Kant's works as they gradually appeared in the 1780s and 1790s not just as academic treatises but as harbingers of a new order' (Pinkard 2002: 84). The reason can be gleaned from Schelling's exalted cry in 1795: 'The beginning and end of all philosophy is freedom' (Schelling 1980: 67). There is no need for a political pursuit and institutional support of liberty; Kant offers instead an overriding conception of freedom modelled on three areas of autonomy: critical reason, the individual, and the faculty of philosophy. These self-regulating areas represent the possibility of an autonomy that is not directly and explicitly political but rather counter-political: it promises that a more authentic politics awaits elsewhere. Freedom is intimately tied to ethics through the moral idea of autonomy, 'that is, the property which will has of being a law to itself' (Kant 1964: 114). Freedom understood as autonomy means individual self-governance. Individuals establish their inner law, an action-guiding morality which rejects the demands of externally imposed obedience and declares itself free. This view of morality has deep roots in the early eighteenth century:

Kant was raised on the Wolffian view that knowledge can make at least some of us self-governing, and in the writings of Rousseau as well as the British moralists he had seen richer and more egalitarian conceptions of self-governance. His own work emerged from consideration of several alternatives to earlier conceptions of morality as obedience.

Schneewind 1998: 509

In the *Critique of Pure Reason* (1781), Kant distinguishes between *dogmatism*, where reason takes a set of principles for granted, and *scepticism*, where reason examines its operations and reflects on its dogmatic attachments. The book charts a course of thought between the dominant Wolffian *rationalism* and the threatening Humean *empiricism* by suggesting that, as a new science, its critical philosophy (which is concerned with the transcendental laws of human knowledge) affords a synthesis of their best elements in an attempt to establish how subjective conditions of thought may have objective validity: it provides a critique of knowledge with a view to the establishment of the conditions of legitimacy of its statements. Kant defends the objective order of things against sceptical empiricism, not through subjectless rationalism but through the subject's own experience and productive activity. The third and last section of the First Critique, 'Transcendental Dialectic', deals with the consequences of the limitations inherent in knowledge, and includes a discussion of the three forms of dialectical conclusions of reason. One of these forms is the four antinomies of pure reason, that is, equally valid but conflicting claims about the world which transcendental reason attempts to reconcile. In each antinomy, the thesis constitutes the doctrine of philosophical dogmatism while the antithesis expresses the teaching of philosophical empiricism. The famous third or relational antinomy between freedom and necessity consists in the following. We can assert that freedom of will initiates its causal history, and therefore that we are radically free to determine our actions. We can also assert that there is a cause for every event, and therefore that we are beings obeying the laws of a determinist nature. The thesis of the antinomy claims that, to explain the appearance of beings in the world, we need to assume, beyond the laws of nature, a prior causality, that of freedom. The antithesis of the antinomy contradicts the thesis by positing that everything is determined by all-powerful natural laws, and the existence of freedom would contradict the law of causality, and even lead to lawlessness.

As a reader of Rousseau and himself an Enlightenment thinker, Kant is concerned with the ability to follow moral imperatives. He asks how humans as sensuous beings in the realm of appearance are determined by natural laws and at the same time function as free agents who are responsible for their deeds. Individuals wonder whether their actions can be free or are compelled by nature and predetermined by fate. If the former applies, responsibility is available; if the latter, morality is impossible. Practical reason, which is the rational capacity for self-determination, must either depend on something absolute or itself be something absolute. How can a foundational principle be legitimate when internal legitimacy may appear arbitrary and external legitimacy cancels its founding character? Kant provides valid proofs for both positions, showing that they are equally based on pure reason. Therefore their conflict is a necessary antagonism within reason which cannot be abolished. An antinomy may be resolved but cannot be removed. Is there then a legitimate basis of autonomy?

Kant takes freedom to be an 'absolute spontaneity', a radical origin that starts a series of causes and effects but is itself an absolute beginning because it does not have a cause. He does not claim to show the actuality of freedom but only its intelligibility, or, rather, its intelligible causality. Since its reality cannot be proved by reference to natural laws, freedom cannot be demonstrated, cannot be a concept of experience or an object of full comprehension. It is a mere idea of reason whose possibility we need to defend if we are to conceive a being as rational and capable of responsibility. By suggesting that this antinomy has no theoretical resolution and is ultimately inexplicable, Kant makes freedom the great problem of his era in German thought in general.

He resolves the antinomy by proposing that, as phenomena in the empirical world, we are determined by nature but, as noumena in the intelligible world, we are free because we can act on the basis of an 'ought' which posits how things should be. This resolution guides his effort to ground a moral theory in a contingent world with no traditional divine authority, and produces the content-less, formalist categorical imperative which acknowledges the autonomy of a self-legislating society. Transcendental freedom makes it possible for rational agents to assume practical freedom. There is an intrinsic connection between self-determination and morality. A free will is a moral will. An autonomous agent acts on a principle that can be supported by the rational standard of an imperative based on self-given law. In the practical sphere, we must think of ourselves as free, and conceive of the laws governing our actions as self-imposed rather than ordained from outside. Although we cannot prove our freedom on theoretical grounds, we must presuppose it on practical grounds so that we can defend self-direction.

The will is subject to the law but in such a way that it must be considered as also giving the law to itself: we are subject only to self-created norms. 'Kantian autonomy presupposes that we are rational agents whose transcendental freedom takes us out of the domain of natural causation. It belongs to every individual, in the state of nature as well as in society. Through it each person has a compass that enables "common human reason" to tell what is consistent with duty and what inconsistent. Our moral capacities are made known to each of us by the fact of reason, our awareness of a categorical obligation that we can respect against the pull of desire' (Schneewind 1998: 515). Giving binding imperatives to oneself requires a special kind of self-determination, namely, giving the practical law to oneself. Freedom can be truly achieved only by overcoming the sensuous elements which characterize man as a being determined by natural causality, and by following instead the self-imposed laws of reason. This requires not only vigilance but also a constant struggle between passion and principle so that temptation can be resisted and desire kept under rational control. If one gives the law to oneself because one accepts it as what one ought to do, then this subject is truly free, reconciling freedom (of choice) with necessity (of obedience) in ethical self-determination or 'free necessity' (Novalis 1997: 93-4). This is the self-legislation of autonomy, which means becoming subject to one's own yet universal moral legislation. Autonomy requires freedom but is not identical to it. Autonomy consists in freedom willing the moral law in that it combines acting freely and acting dutifully. We are self-governing because we are autonomous.

The laws which agents give themselves appear from one angle prior to self-legislation and from another posterior to it because rational creatures enable reason to have a claim on them and to make them act as moral agents.

This raises the question of normativity. 'The most obvious difficulty in Kant's approach was also clearly seen by Kant himself: how do we explain the way in which we are both *subject* to the norms of reason and yet also the agents who *institute* those norms? How, after all, can we actually be *bound* by laws we *make*? In particular, Kant's conception required some account of how "we" institute norms and whether the norms making up what we call "reason" are not "instituted" by us at all but simply are what they are' (Pinkard 2002: 67). The turning point came when Kant made aesthetics the privileged domain for the understanding and practice of autonomy. By examining the legitimacy of aesthetic judgments in the *Critique of Judgement* (1790), he investigated ways in which we are subject to norms we ourselves institute. How do we make judgments about the beautiful and communicate them to other rational beings, expecting them to have the same response, even though they involve not rules but subjective taste? What is the source of the normative demand for agreement in matters of taste? How do judgments of taste acquire their intersubjective validity? The experience of the beautiful cannot be explained in terms of concepts based on rules but as the ability for aesthetic taste structured by universal norms. Taste consists not in stating norms of beauty but in a capacity for aesthetic appreciation. This shared capacity savours harmony, the way things fit according to no particular purpose. Shaftesbury had already assumed an analogy between moral distinctions and aesthetic judgments. When well educated, the moral faculty can reveal true harmony to us by showing how objects constitute a harmonious whole. Accordingly, virtuous agents need no external command as they strive to become the architects of their own fortune, shaping themselves so that their lives achieve the kind of harmony that deserves moral approval. Building on this tradition while adding to it the Pietist concerns with character and education, Kant sees an isomorphism between empirical feelings of moral responsibility and those of aesthetic pleasure which we know are necessary even though there is no theoretical accounting for them. He turned to aesthetics to solve what he had come to recognize as crucial problems *for morality*: how the rational idea of autonomy that underlies morality – that is, the ideal of self-governance by the free choice always to act in accordance with the universal law of pure reason – ... can be made palpable to fully embodied rational agents like ourselves, and how this ideal of pure reason can nevertheless lead to a set of duties that do not just ignore the sensuous aspect of our being but include it.

Guyer 1993: 19

Aesthetic ideology presents art as the phenomenal manner in which the spirit knows and represents itself, articulating this self-awareness in form, in ethical judgment. Kant claims that 'the beautiful is the symbol of the morally good' (Kant 1978: 223). Aesthetic pleasure has a deep moral significance as an experience of freedom because, as a disinterested attitude, it is free of cognitive or practical constrains. While the majority of British and German thinkers in the eighteenth century sought to justify the interest in beauty by grounding aesthetic pleasure in cognitive and practical interests, Kant argues that 'it is only by means of its detachment from any direct service of the interests of reason that aesthetic experience can more indirectly serve these interests by providing us with a sensible image of our freedom itself and of the primacy of practical reason; the disinterestedness of our delight in the beautiful is itself that which serves the interest of reason' (Guyer 1933: 92-3). Judgments of taste serve the interests of morality by virtue of their disinterestedness: the freedom of aesthetic experience prepares for the practice of moral freedom. When released from moral didacticism and political ideology, aesthetic autonomy promotes practical reason. Kant explores links between freedom and nature by analysing how aesthetic judgment connects cognitive and ethical capacities in that it identifies objects which generate a harmonious play of understanding and imagination, thus providing feelings of pleasure. The freedom of judgment from extrinsic norms when determining beauty in the material world is analogous to the freedom of practical reason from heteronomous constraints when it determines our intentions in the natural world. Beauty (which Edmund Burke called 'a social quality') bridges the gap between the cognitive understanding of natural law and the practical reason facing moral tasks.

Kant's ethical turn, which produced out of the original 'Critique of Taste' (1787) the finished *Critique of Judgement*, extends his aesthetics and establishes an analogy between beauty and morality, making possible the aesthetic resolution later sought by the Idealists. 'At this point what needs to be noted is that the conviction that the work of art owes itself in a fundamental way to freedom and thus provides the most direct route to the task of thinking and preserving freedom defines the origins of German Idealism and will shape its development to come' (Schmidt 2001: 82). What started as a systematic exposition of the faculty of judgment ends up as an attempt to reconcile in a transcendent unity the 'sensible realm' of nature and necessity with the 'suprasensible realm' of will and freedom. Still, because it is limited to the will, self-determination remains an ethical issue, and self-governance based on moral autonomy alone. Instead of liberty, Kant is pursuing universal moral legislation. To some degree Lucien Goldmann was right to call him a tragic philosopher since it was on the basis of his dichotomies that Idealism identified freedom with absolute Ego, understood the tragic as the affirmation of Ego's freedom, and posited beauty born out of dialectical conflict as the unification of necessity and freedom.

Building on Kant's argument in the Third Critique about the capacity of beauty to reconcile natural law and practical reason, necessity and responsibility, Schiller will propose art, the domain of aesthetics proper, as a means for the 'aesthetic education of man'. The aesthetic fuses the incommensurable claims of subjectivity and nature. The competing demands of moral cognition and scientific knowledge are suspended once aesthetic reason responds to compelling artworks. Through the mediation of art, freedom and necessity may reach a synthesis since beauty represents the material expression of autonomy. Through art, objects become unique works and are experienced as creations with their own normative claims. They are the sensual products of freedom that triumph over mechanical causality. Consequently, through an aesthetic education self-determination will act artistically on the self. Instead of compelling people with imperatives, art, as a product of free human initiative, will train them in morality through pleasure. Kant's idea of harmony becomes an ideal of justice and political stability. Artworks constitute realizations of freedom and articulations of wholeness in a world threatened by submissiveness and fragmentation. Art emerges as a realm of reconciliation that is able to suspend the negative effects of the functional differentiation of society.

Between the evils of oppressive despotism and revolutionary anarchy, Kant proposes a moral hegemony modelled on the conciliatory promise of aesthetic autonomy. To that effect, he pursues the universalization of the moral imperative by placing the law not in abstract duty but in the self-regulating structures of a subjectivity which, like autonomous art, gives the law to itself. His successors will deal with far more complex cases where moral imperatives compete in the framework of ethical antinomy. The egalitarian sphere of public taste will gaze into the dark depth of modern subjectivity which embraces the law as the very principle of autonomy, and polices its desires accordingly. At this juncture, the tragic idea emerges as precisely what escapes Kant's transcendental reason – the unresolvable antinomy, the self-destructive autonomy, the contradictory self-legislation, the differentiation that cannot be sublated. With it, appear several pressing questions: how can an interiorized emancipation escape internalized repression? What happens when the demands of self-governance begin to impede self-determination? Above all, can freedom defy the rule of autonomy?

Friedrich Schiller (1793)

The first law of the tragic art was to represent suffering nature.
The second law is to represent the resistance of morality opposed
to suffering.

Schiller 1902: 152

Despite his first major theatrical achievements with the tragedies
The Robbers (1781), *The Conspiracy of Fiesco in Genoa* (1782) and
Intrigue and Love (1783), Friedrich Schiller (1759-1805) reaches a
creative impasse at the end of the 1780s with the unwieldy artistic
and political demands of the tragedy *Don Carlos* (1787), his meeting
with Goethe (1788), his appointment as Professor of History at the
University of Jena (1789) and his systematic study of Kant's *Critique
of Judgement* (1790). So long as he has full confidence in the stage as
moral institution (its works, its public and its support), he goes on
composing grand and successful tragedies. As the 'Storm and Stress'
period begins to come to its early end, and as the French Revolution
takes its intellectual toll, Schiller turns to historical and philosophical studies, and abandons tragedy for a decade, until 1799. During
this period he publishes two historical books, translates Euripides,
Virgil, Racine and Shakespeare, and produces his great essays, dras-
tically revising the role of modern art. In the words of Thomas Mann,
those were the 'years of penance which this powerful artist imposed
on himself, the years of philosophical speculation, aesthetic metaphysics, and criticism during which he sternly renounced poetic
creativity for the sake of freedom' (Mann 1958: 16).

In the first essays of this period, Schiller distinguishes aesthetic
from moral qualities, giving priority to the former and pleading for
the independence of art. He also proclaims tragedy the paradigmatic
art form and, through a reconsideration of pity, gives moral valida-
tion to aesthetic pleasure. To the extent that he investigates
emotional effect and explores the contribution of theatre to the moral
edification of the national audience, he remains a Neo-classical

follower of Lessing. However, in analysing the incompatibility of aims (the paradox of tragedy) and the conflict of physical and moral proprieties, he gradually discovers discord at the heart of tragedy.

In the essay 'On the Cause of the Pleasure We Derive from Tragic Objects' (1792), he posits that the free pleasure of art 'rests wholly upon moral conditions, and all the moral faculties of man are exercised in it' (Schiller 1902: 368). The source of all pleasure is 'propriety, the conformity with the aim' (370). When this propriety is manifested by means of a law of nature, it results in sensual pleasure; when it is manifested by means of a law of reason (the good) and imagination (the beautiful), it results in moral pleasure. 'This moral propriety is never more vividly recognized than when it is found in conflict with another propriety, and still keeps the upper hand; then only the moral law awakens in full power, when we find it struggling against all the other forces of nature, and when all those forces lose in their presence their empire over a human soul. ... It follows that the highest degree of moral consciousness can only exist in strife, and the highest moral pleasure is always accompanied by pain' (373). Tragedy is poetry that secures a high degree of moral pleasure through mixed emotions, sacrificing a physical propriety to a moral one or a moral propriety to a higher one (374). It is the highest moral propriety as a principle of tragic emotion that elicits pleasure in tragic objects. Nature and morality find their fitting combination in tragic pleasure.

In the subsequent essay 'On the Tragic Art' (1792), the discord between physical and moral proprieties begins to take on a different form, the strife between freedom and necessity. The balance between agreeable and disagreeable affections 'depends on the proportion between the moral nature and the sensuous nature of man' (348). The sources of pleasure in sad affection are the sympathetic pleasures of tragic pity emanating from our moral nature. As the previous essay established, 'in every tragic emotion there is an idea of incongruity, which ... must always lead on to the conception of a higher consistency' (352). The incongruity between sensuous and moral nature must rest on a deeper unity. The discontent caused by the contradiction between destiny and freedom must be resolved by a consciousness of higher harmony. 'This happens when the very discontent with destiny becomes effaced, and is resolved in a presen-

31

timent or rather a clear consciousness of a teleological concatenation of things, of a sublime order, of a beneficent will. Then to the pleasure occasioned in us by moral consistency is joined the invigorating idea of the most perfect suitability in the great whole of nature' (355). The initial challenge to an order which caused pain proves a stimulus to reason for the discovery of general laws which justify the particular case by placing its discord 'in the centre of the general harmony' (355). In fact this may be the only area where modern art can surpass ancient: 'Greek art never rose to this supreme serenity of tragic motion, because neither the national religion, nor even the philosophy of the Greeks, lighted their step on this advanced road' (355). Thus by enabling contemporary theatre to surpass the classical, tragic discontent promises to reconcile the Moderns with the Ancients. Having reached this conclusion, the essay reverts in its second half to normative poetics, outlining first the basic features of tragic art, and then the conditions under which the pleasure of tragic emotion can be produced with greatest force. Although in the piece Schiller probes for the first time the tragic paradox in terms of fate and self-determination, he is more interested in essential harmony than transitional discontent. The teleology of wholeness where everything fits gives cosmic law priority over any civic or personal law.

The question of aesthetic and moral judgment remains central (169) in the essay 'The Pathetic' of the following year. But the subject is no longer the moral character of aesthetic pleasure, as was the case in the earlier essays. From the beginning, this one focuses on the struggle for freedom. Suffering is identified as a special quality which arises out of mortal conflict between the rights of nature (necessity) and the rights of reason (moral freedom). When sensuous nature stirs man and he tries to maintain his freedom of the soul, we have that special passion, the pathetic, which is represented in tragedy. Affections, especially painful ones, are still the larger context of Schiller's inquiry. But this time at issue is not the paradox of tragic pleasure but the paradox of tragic ethics: the moral force of man overcomes suffering in sustaining its independence because moral man maintains himself independently of natural laws. For the principle of freedom to become conscious of itself, it needs to offer resistance; for resistance to arise, nature must attack man with all its power. Here, Kant's third antinomy between the necessity of freedom and the freedom of necessity takes centre stage transformed from a moral antinomy of reason to the tragic paradox of human action. 'Throughout moral liberty we require the human being who suffers; throughout all the sufferings of human nature we always desire to perceive the independent spirit, or the capacity for independence' (164). In the essay 'On the Tragic Art', Schiller had outlined the conditions for tragic art, which followed from how pity is successfully solicited. Here, he outlines the two conditions in every kind of the pathetic: '1st. Suffering, to interest our sensuous nature; 2nd. Moral liberty, to interest our spiritual nature' (164). Gradually, as matters of the audience recede into the background, the study focuses on the tragic quality of tragic art, in this case defined as 'the pathetic'. 'In this way, Schiller first formulated a view of the tragic as a fundamental feature of human existence, indicative of the irremediable, painful incompatibility between the individual and the world in which he or she happens to find himself or herself ... and then, in a second step, assigned to the genre of tragedy the mission of adequately embodying this insight' (Most 2000: 31). The turning point can be dated to 1793, which was also the year of Schiller's letters to C.G. Körner outlining 'Kallias', the unfinished treatise on the beautiful.

At the same time as the emphasis on the tragic quality of tragedy intensifies, the distance between the aesthetic and the moral widens. Kant proposed that, if the highest service of the experience of beauty to the needs of morality is to offer humanity a palpable experience of freedom, then the encounter with beauty must be protected from the constraints of concepts, including moral ones. Only when morality recognizes aesthetic autonomy does taste serve moral autonomy. Schiller takes this a step further, differentiating radically between the two judgments. Based on imagination and oriented towards (dis)pleasure, the aesthetic judgment requires freedom of the soul. Based on reason and oriented towards (dis)approbation, the moral judgment requires the good. This distinction reinforces the opposition between subjective freedom and objective necessity: 'The liberty of the imagination would be fettered by too great respect for the moral law; and violence would be done to the character of *necessity* which is in the reason, in missing the *liberty* which belongs to the imagination' (Schiller 1902: 174). The two judgments are not complementary – on the contrary, 'the moral judgment and the aesthetic, far from mutually corroborating each other, impede and hinder each other, because they impress on the soul two directions entirely opposite. In fact, this observance of rule which reason requires of us as moral judge is incompatible with the independence which the imagination calls for as aesthetic judge' (170). Thus we reach here the first major affirmation of the aesthetic as an autonomous, superior and liberating force. Only art acts on the whole of human nature, only the aesthetic judgment leaves us free, only imagination delivers us from necessity.

The origins of dialectical thought lie in a certain interpretation of tragedy which forsakes first the crafts of the stage and then the education of the public to concentrate on a speculative theatre and ultimately on an abstract quality called the Tragic. Already within Schiller's own work during 1790-2, the quest for catharsis moves from Lessing's Aristotelian inquiry into the audience to the contradictions of Kantian critique as a positive hermeneutic activity. The playwright's response to the Third Critique sets the stage for a thorough thematization of tragedy. Pursuing an intellectual, counter-political revolution, Schiller struggles with the Kantian distinctions between freedom and necessity, understanding and sense, and mind and nature, producing his own cumulative differentiations between spirit and sense, form and life, form drive and sense drive, reflective and naïve art, and the like. Establishing a dialectical perspective, he is constantly concerned with self-division – the divided self, existence, reality, tradition, loyalties, etc. – and is searching for the totality that would overcome national belatedness and social fragmentation. When the self-opposing activity of self-consciousness is taken as the generating centre, the tragic itself emerges not as the transcendence but as the very affirmation and embracing of such a disjuncture, and takes on the expression of a revolt of the free will against fate. What had begun in the early 1780s as an inquiry into contemporary German theatre as a moral institution, where the domain of law ends and the jurisdiction of the stage begins (Schiller 1959: 265), developed into the first modern aesthetic theory and concluded twenty years later with a tragic view of the will, or rather, a theory of the tragic creative act which unifies will and fate. The search for the right combination of Lessing's moral instruction and Kant's disinterested pleasure produced a resounding affirmation of the unfettered ethics of the aesthetic judgment.

When Kant asked how we can be bound by our own laws, he found a model in the republic of taste and proposed the aesthetic judgment as a paradigm of counter-political civics. Elaborating on this, Schiller argues that the best place for this exercise is a republic of self-forma-tion where the tragic perils of autonomy (the uncertainties of liberty) can be bypassed by the disinterested ethics of art. The aesthetic phenomenon constitutes an objectification of human essence, which is rational morality: in the artwork, freedom becomes objective to itself. 'Beauty, or rather taste, regards all things as *ends in them-selves* and will not permit one to serve as the purpose of another, or to be under its control. Everyone is a free citizen and has the same rights as the most noble in the world of aesthetics, coercion may not take place even *for the sake of the whole* – everyone must *consent*' (Schiller 2003: 170). Thus aesthetic politics first arrives with the claim that beauty is freedom incarnate. That is why Schiller describes beauty in terms of both freedom and self-limitation, both power and self-restriction. Schiller completes the philosophical emancipation of the aesthetic judgment from cognitive and moral determination, defending the independence of beauty from ratio-nalist cognition and religious morality, and envisioning an art that does not serve any melioristic purposes. Thus in the span of the same century German thought moves from the Wolffian police state to the Kantian legal state to the Schillerian aesthetic one.

The concepts of the aesthetic and the tragic emerge together and define the parameters of dialectical understanding. They emerge in Germany during the shift from a national audience to a theatre audi-ence, as the didactic emphasis on the moral and public role of literature fades across much of Western Europe under the demands of 'affective individualism' for aesthetic pleasure. They represent the affirmative and the negative side of the collective retreat from the self-legislation of freedom towards the self-limitation of autonomy, which consists of freedom willing the moral law and acting dutifully. In this historico-philosophical sense, Idealist philosophy itself is part of the German dramatic tradition and theory. Schiller is the key figure in the effort to create such a tradition. It is with the next generation of writers, and especially with Hölderlin, Schiller's desperate reader, that the tragic will leave the stage of speculative tragedy and begin to lead a life of its own. This departure will conclude the great Idealist evolution towards what Schiller in the *Kallias Letters* called *Heautonomie* (self-determination as inner necessity) – national, political, individual and artistic, all of them modelled on the aesthetic state (as defined in the twenty-first of the *Letters on the Aesthetic Education of Mankind* in 1795), itself based on Winckelmann's vision of aesthetic Hellas (Chytry 1989: 91).

> Posa's speech [in *Don Carlos*] and the trumpet signal in Beethoven's *Fidelio* [1805] are signs of hope and of political impotence at the same time. To be sure, the autonomy of art and its utopian vision keeps the ideals of humanity alive, but in the context of German history, i.e. of failed revolutions, they were increasingly relegated to the aesthetic sphere where art could be celebrated without having practical consequences. ... The German tradition of freedom of thought and of an aesthetic revolution has imprisoned freedom: it has become an internalized aesthetic experience.
>
> Berghahn 1992: 115-16

With his great essays of 1792-5, which culminate in the aesthetic writings at the end of the Jacobin experiment in late 1794, Schiller concludes the immense transition from the empirical poetics of drama to a fully-fledged philosophy of tragedy, and prepares the way for the metaphysics of the Tragic, which the other Jena Romantics will develop during the rest of that decade.

Friedrich Wilhelm Schelling (1795)

> Greek tragedy honored human freedom, letting its hero *fight*
> against the superior power of fate. … It was a *sublime* thought,
> to suffer punishment willingly even for an inevitable crime, and
> so to prove one's freedom by the very loss of this freedom, and
> to go down with a declaration of free will. Here too, as in all
> instances, Greek art is *standard* [Regel].
>
> Schelling 1980: 193

Schiller believed that art releases humans from the shackles of
nature/necessity and that 'aesthetic education' enables them to exercise their free will. In beauty, sense and reason reach harmony. And
yet he sensed that somewhere beyond this realm of balanced joy and
pain limits are overstepped, contrary attitudes clash, the spirit is
reached, and the idea captured. In the essay 'On the Sublime' (1801),
he exclaims: 'Away then with that false theory which supposes falsely
a harmony binding well being and well doing. Let evil destiny show
its face. Our safety is not in blindness, but in facing our dangers'
(Schiller 1902: 148). As a fellow dramatist and thinker noted in 1959,
'in the world of non-nature freedom becomes something tragic'
(Dürrenmatt 1976: 109). This is the heroic search for the tragic itself,
which Schiller calls by several names (the pathetic, the sublime,
dignity, liberty) but truly and memorably defined for generations to
come. Peter Szondi's (2002) study of the tragic reiterated the argument of his teacher, Emil Staiger, that the beginning of tragic theory
lies in the tenth of Schelling's *Philosophical Letters on Dogmatism
and Criticism* (1795). However, it would have been more accurate to
say that in the years 1795-1802, Schelling, Hölderlin and Hegel all
publish on tragic art, pursuing paths first opened by Schiller.

For example, in that last Letter, the twenty-year-old Schelling
(1775-1854) returns to Schiller's inquiry into the 'paradox of
tragedy', namely, its ability to elicit pleasure from pain: 'Many a time
the question has been asked how Greek reason could bear the contra-

dictions of Greek tragedy' (Schelling 1980: 192). Here is one such contradiction: 'A mortal, destined by fate to become a malefactor and himself fighting *against* this fate, is nevertheless appallingly punished for the crime, although it was the deed of destiny!' (192). This suffering represents an intolerable injustice. What made it bearable 'lay in the contest between human freedom and the power of the objective world' (192) and the way tragedy recognized and honoured that freedom. Specifically, tragedy highlighted the capacity of the tragic hero to admit to a crime that is the result of destiny and to embrace the fate of a criminal. Schelling's Letter asserts that the fight against the necessity of the objective power affirms individual freedom, a struggle preserved in art. For Schiller, it was man's moral force that fought nature, overcame suffering and sustained the independence of his soul. Schelling introduces the dimension of guilt by understanding freedom as absolute 'I' and necessity as crime. His model (like Aristotle's) is Oedipus, who is destined for crime and punished for his revolt against necessity. His story provides criticism with its master plot: 'In criticism, my vocation is to strive for immutable selfhood, unconditional freedom, unlimited activity. Be! is the supreme demand of criticism' (192).

Schelling rejects the self-imposed laws of Kantian reason and embraces the superior logic of antinomianism, of revolt against the laws of necessity. As a post-Schillerian, he is not interested so much in tragic effect as in the aesthetic experience of the tragic, transposing the paradox from the stage to human fate. 'What made the contradictions of which their tragedies were woven bearable to the Greeks was not principally some "effect" of restored harmony or the purification of certain effects which would permit one to substitute pleasure for painful emotions, but, more fundamentally, the fact that the spectator's catharsis points to this reconciliation which is at work in tragedy itself, a reconciliation of which tragedy constitutes, as it were, the unequalled *event*' (Courtine 1993: 162). Criticism consults Greek reason: How did it bear the contradictions of tragedy? How did it handle the antinomy of doomed freedom? The question is now raised in the realm of individual identity.

Freedom is confirmed not by resistance despite suffering, as in Schiller, but by a willed fall. The tragic is the confirmation of a defiant will. By willingly accepting punishment for an inevitable crime, man is able to exert his whole freedom and go down with a declaration of free will. To prove freedom in the very loss of it 'means to see existence through Protestant eyes. The paradox is the Protestant paradox *par excellence* (even if we may also detect it elsewhere, as in Kafka's conception of guilt). It lies at the root of the theologies of Luther and Kierkegaard' (Silk 1980: 308). If Kant thought that a free will is a moral one, Schelling believes that a free will is a guilty one that maintains its moral integrity. Freedom consists not in the self-governance of autonomy but in the futile revolt of autonomy against heteronomy. In the Protestant view, 'Greek drama is enacted in the existential space between the omnipotent and mysterious ordinance of the transcendent gods and man's situation wholly at the mercy of that ordinance; and again, between the necessity-stricken and wholly unfree physical being of man (the physical being at the mercy of what Kant had called the blind forces of nature) and the triumphant, wholly spiritual and inward "freedom" of the will and the moral intention, whose workings are entirely independent of a man's material and physical nature' (309). When guilt becomes necessary and defiant, when fate turns guilty and heroic, the tragic is born, finding its incarnation in a hero who is responsible for a certain crime (and not just an error) yet ethically innocent. This approach takes Oedipus as its prototype. The meaning of the tragic, dialectically defined, is the affirmation of freedom through the contradictory figure of the hero who chooses to be responsible for all that he has done (instead of attributing it to destiny) because this is for him the best path to absolute freedom even though it leads to death or some other catastrophe.

The tragic antinomies of Idealism offer a dialectical resolution to the fundamental speculative contradiction between the subjective (absolute I) and the objective (absolute Not-I) represented by criticism and dogmatism, liberty and necessity, art and nature. Schelling asked: 'How was Greek reason (i.e., basically, how was philosophy ...) able to 'purify' itself of the menace which the contradiction illustrated by the tragic conflict represented?' (Lacoue-Labarthe 1978: 66). His answer was that the subject claims its freedom by its very loss. Tragedy maintains the contradiction since the hero is both guilty and innocent in struggling against a destiny that bears responsibility for his fault. Reconciliation operates within the tragic logic of the identity of identity and difference. As a conciliatory presentation of the contradictions of Kantian reason, tragedy represents the supreme 'catharsis of the speculative' (81).

A few years later (in 1802-3), Schelling delivers his lectures on *The Philosophy of Art* at the University of Jena, where in 1798 at age twenty-three he succeeded Fichte. Here he presents drama as the 'final synthesis' of a conflict between epic and lyric poetry, 'a higher identity ... which by encompassing the characteristics of the other two antithetical genres is the highest manifestation of the nature and essence of all art' (Schelling 1989: 247). If the fundamental antithesis between the finite and the infinite finds its highest artistic expression in the conflict between necessity and freedom, then drama reconciles the necessity dominating epic and the freedom dominating lyric poetry. 'Since *freedom* and *necessity* are the *highest* expressions of that particular antithesis upon which all art is based, the highest manifestation of art is thus the one in which necessity is victorious without freedom succumbing, and in a reverse fashion in which freedom triumphs without necessity being overcome' (249). As Schelling admits, this definition deduces drama as tragedy (251). Furthermore, it presents tragedy as a double synthesis, a synthesis of both freedom and necessity (as in the *Philosophical Letters*, which Schelling himself cites in *The Philosophy of Art*) and of the epic and lyric genres of poetry. The ultimate concern of tragedy is the 'equilibrium between justice and humanity' (255) represented by the fall of the hero. What is tragic is that 'this guiltless guilty person accepts punishment voluntarily [and] thereby alone does freedom transfigure itself into the highest identity with necessity' (255).

Freedom can be achieved only through self-cancellation, affirmation can be realized only through self-denial. Read in light of *The Philosophy of Art*, the view that freedom materializes in self-immolation, first expressed in the tenth Letter, becomes an aesthetic-apocalyptic argument: autonomy cannot materialize – it can only happen. 'As Schelling's remarks make clear this is a demand made by the aesthetic form of a work of art. By being an aesthetic object, the work of art thus becomes the place in which the history of freedom is written as the limiting of freedom' (Ferris 2000: 99). Schiller concluded that only art acts on the whole of human nature, only the aesthetic judgment leaves humans free, only imagination delivers them from necessity. Schelling agrees that the best model of freedom is aesthetic, that the aesthetic is the model of freedom.

Friedrich Hölderlin (1800)

The declining fatherland, nature and man, insofar as they bear a particular relation of reciprocity, insofar as they constitute a special world which has become ideal and [constitute] a union of things and insofar as they dissolve, so that from the world and from the remaining ancestry and forces of nature, which are the other real principle, there emerge a new world, a new yet also particular reciprocal relation just as that decline emerged from a pure yet particular world.

Hölderlin 1988: 96

Thus writes Schelling's close friend, Friedrich Hölderlin (1770-1843), in his essay 'Becoming in Dissolution' in 1800. In an attempt to account for the Kantian opposition between freedom and necessity, Idealism produces the idea of the tragic, promising that in the dialectical course of events conflict is resolved through aesthetic reconciliation whereby beauty represents the unification of the two forces. The notion mesmerizes Hölderlin, and quickly takes him beyond his early Kantian worries over the 'law of freedom' (33) and the 'law of morality' (36). The essay 'On the Difference of Poetic Modes' (1798) is an unfinished effort to define the distinct character of epic, lyric and tragic poetry. Hölderlin treats tragedy as poetic metaphor for philosophy. Here he develops the programme of Idealism around the tragic idea. The tragic is founded on the intellectual intuition of the 'unity within everything living'. This unity results from 'the impossibility of an absolute separation and individuation' and at the same time from the need for different modes of union and the subsequent differentiating movement of its parts. The whole must split into parts so that the potential of both whole and parts may be fulfilled. Hölderlin explains that separation and union 'are only a state of the primordially united, a state wherein it exists because it had to transcend itself due to the stasis which could not occur in it because its mode of union could not always stay the same with regard to matter, because parts of the united must not always remain in the same closer and remoter relation, so that everything may encounter everything else and that all receive its full right and share of life, and that every part during its course equal the whole in completeness' (Hölderlin 1988: 84-5).

At a certain point, separation supervenes and disrupts the unity. The primal whole enters the state of division because every part must attain its full measure of life and all must meet all. It is the dissolution of stasis that makes completeness accessible. 'The unity present in the intellectual intuition manifests itself as a sensuous one precisely to the extent that it transcends itself, that the separation of its parts occurs which, too, separate only because they feel too unified' (85). As each part becomes complete as a whole, and the parts become totally individual and separate, tragedy occurs at the point of maximum disunity. In this excess of spirit within unity, in its search for transcendence, in its struggle for materiality, 'in this striving for separation of the divisible infinite, which in the state of highest unity of everything organic imparts itself to all parts contained by this unity, in this necessary *arbitrariness of Zeus* there actually lies the ideal beginning of the real separation' (86). The overabundance of unity, the self-transcendence of spirit, the division of completeness bring about the dismemberment of the primordial. However, tragedy is only one, transitional stage of development. 'From here the separation proceeds until the parts are in their most extreme tension, where they resist one another most strongly. From this conflict, it returns into itself, namely, where the parts ... cancel one another, and a new unity originates' (86). In due time, this unity too will produce its feeling of excess and point of disruption. The entire idea of union in division invokes the Heraclitean cosmic order (*logos*) which, while differing (*diapheron*), agrees (*homologeei*) with itself (*heauto*).

The turn from tragedy to the tragic finds its completion in the essays he writes (or, rather, drafts) while working on his most ambitious project, the tragedy *The Death of Empedocles* (1797-9). In 'On the Difference of Poetic Modes', Hölderlin tries to identify the distinct character of this poetic mode, applying the Heraclitean principle of self-differentiation elaborated in *Hyperion*. Primordial unity, in order to avoid the stasis of sameness, cancels and at the same time transcends itself through division, thus reaching materiality and achieving incarnation. Since judgment divides (Fichte 1992: 403), identity (of self with self) is the work of judgment and requires separation: judgment separates empirical self from transcendental self. Being is not identity but what is lost when identity is gained. If being is lost through reflection, it can be glimpsed again only in art. The intuition of the absent being, of lost total unity, constitutes the tragic. 'This explicates the dark side of Schiller: self-consciousness is grounded in an originary unity from which it is necessarily separated. Tragedy thus reveals *the necessity and impossibility* of the unity of freedom with nature' (Bernstein 2003: xxvi). To comprehend this movement of necessary separation *and* impossible individuation, and to accept that oneness is multiple, is to grasp the 'arbitrariness of Zeus', the tragic essence of the *hen* (one).

The essay 'The "Ground" for Empedocles' (1799) discusses tragedy as the drama of interiority which 'always denies and must deny its ultimate foundation' (Hölderlin 1988: 51). The 'tragic-dramatic poem' unfolds as the dialectic between the organic/reflective and the aorgic/unreflective principle within the protagonist who is portrayed as a poet contemplating totality. The poet's responsibility is to reconcile the opposition between the organic and the aorgic, art and nature. The essay begins with the cardinal idea of 'excess' within unity and the search for transcendence already encountered in the previous essay. This time, the originary and differentiating discord is 'the excess of inwardness' (50). For the artistic man's understanding of *harmonia* (a word in Heraclitean Fragment No. 51) to be known, his life 'must present itself in the excess of inwardness where the opposed principles interchange' (53), a presentation where the arbitrariness of Zeus will inevitably lead to the artist's death. This is the theme of *Empedocles*. At the moment of the poet-philosopher's death, the individuality of aorgic origin becomes again more universal while the universality of organic origin becomes more particular. Thus 'the particular at its extreme must increasingly and actively universalize itself against the extreme of the aorgic ... whereas the aorgic must increasingly concentrate against the extreme of the particular and must gain a centre and become the most particular' (54).

The reconciliation of art and nature involves the interchange of opposite poles. Hölderlin's focus is not on the Empedoclean strife of elements but on the strife that develops between man and nature because of their estrangement. He seeks the reunion of man with the divine and applies Presocratic vocabulary to *Natur* (aorgic) and *Kunst* (organic) to explore the harmony of their opposition and propose that the interchange of the opposite poles results in their reconciliation. To him, the fundamental concern of tragedy is the highest struggle which generates the greatest hostility and makes the reconciliation of contending extremes appear. The organic and the aorgic pass from extreme separation to extreme union and each takes on the character of the other, returning to its true nature. However, in order to intensify, their union needs to dissolve, and therefore demands the poet's sacrifice. In the end, 'the excess of inwardness which emerged by chance – yet originally did so only as an ideal and as an attempt – and which has now become real by way of the highest antagonism, cancels itself, precisely for that reason, the degrees, forces, and mechanisms in which the original excess of inwardness, the cause of all antagonism was cancelled' (56-7). This is what makes the tragic hero a victim of the demands of his epoch whose destiny is individualized in him and his ruin.

The broader idea of an existing world dissolving and a new one emerging returns in the fragment 'Becoming in Dissolution' (1800). Here the earlier concern with tragedy as a genre disappears altogether, and the philosophical exploration of union focuses on the necessity of dissolution. In the context of the reciprocity between nature and man posited in the opening of the essay (see the epigraph of this section), that is to say, in the context of a harmonious conflict of cosmic forces, 'dissolution as such, an existence *per se*, seems more authentic, and the real or the dissolving is comprehended in a state of necessity between being and not being' (Hölderlin 1988: 97). As reality dissolves and finds itself between the two poles, existence is 'felt in its dissolution' (96), 'the possible enters into reality' (97) and, as 'forever-creative', becomes real everywhere. This is the fearless, heroic, daring dissolution which operates as a productive act leading from decline to a new state, the next union, as the following dialectical principle declares: 'at every point of the same there exist dissolution and becoming' (98). The principle expresses a world view which encompasses the supreme reconciliation: 'everything infinitely permeates, touches, and approaches each other in pain and joy, discord and peace, movement and rest, form and formlessness' (98) in a process of boundless transformation. Thus freedom and necessity are reconciled in the liberating need for dissolution, the inescapable and indispensable destruction that alone creates anew, the decline that alone leads to union.

Hölderlin identifies the tragic as the very reciprocity at work here, specifically, as the union of the ideal/individual/finite/old and the real/total/infinite/new in a mythic state (where the epic and the lyric are also united). The inexorable disintegration of the ideal/individual appears as growth while that of the real/total appears as love. Together they constitute a transcendental creative act which fuses the two in a 'tragic union' and produces a new individual striving to isolate and free itself. This dialectic is expressed in a more intense way in the 'Remarks on *Oedipus*' (1803): 'The presentation of the tragic rests primarily on the tremendous – how the god and man mate and how natural force and man's innermost boundlessly unite in wrath – conceiving of itself, [rests] on the boundless union purifying itself through boundless separation' (107).

Hölderlin is certainly indebted to Fichte's view of the reciprocity between self and non-self as a '*coming-to-be through a passing-away* (a becoming through a disappearance)' (Fichte 1982: 165). The subject's legislating capacity and self-authorization become central for Idealism, beginning with Fichte, who makes the self-positing I the source of the intelligibility of the world and the foundation of philosophy. Free action is the principle of Fichte's consciousness. The subject comes into existence as it institutes norms. Conversely, all normative status is instituted by the self. The self acquires its normative status by attributing it to itself. The I constitutes itself as a thinking self in the self-conscious act of normatively positioning itself and authorizing itself to occupy and justify such positions. However, when this absolute I acts upon itself, it becomes divided against itself as it splits into consciousness and the objective world. For most of his life, during successive revisions of his *Science of Knowledge*, Fichte elaborated what the self-positing of the self-authorizing I really meant and to what it was addressed. Hölderlin strips the self of its legislating capacity and instead sees its intrinsic reciprocity as a tragic condition marking human fate and creativity, because in passing-away the 'necessary arbitrariness of Zeus' anni-hilates the tragic figure. Hölderlin's God is a hostile form of nature who moves towards a destructive union with man. The raging hero pits himself against this god who is waiting to 'snatch him into another realm'. When the hero steps into the path of fate, he loses his individuality and suffers divine madness. With this view, Hölderlin's life-long effort to correct the 'errors' of the Greeks by combining their gods with the Christian one collapses and his project comes to a halt, or rather reaches an impasse. Even though he was the first major writer to insist that what he said was what the Greeks had left unsaid, unarticulated, unthought, his creative breakdown suggests that 'perhaps the only tragic heroes a Hesperian (i.e., Christian) poet can create are pre-Socratic Greeks who have read Plato and perform an *imitatio Christi*' (Warminski 1987: 18). This may well be the case for writers who operate within the dialectic of self-realization set out in Schelling's *Philosophical Letters on Dogmatism and Criticism,* especially the moral economy of man's guilt as fated by *Schicksal*/destiny.

'Discordant' (Hölderlin 1988: 131) with himself throughout his career, Hölderlin wavers between a Presocratic cosmology of conflict and a Protestant theology of suffering, and cannot decide whether the final ground for tragedy is philosophical or theological. Thus he removes tragedy from Schiller's moral (catharsis), and later aesthetic (beauty) framework (as Schiller had removed it earlier from that of art criticism), and gives it ontological potency: the unity of conflicting parts does not serve any purpose but acquires its own justification. Other times, he locates tragedy in the poet's life where it becomes a private experience, meaningful in itself – the tragic sense. Thus he moves from the unities of drama to the unity of tragic life, the sacrificial victim of its age. In such a life, the divine mani-fests itself in historical time through its destructive union-in-division with man. At any given moment, Hölderlin produces an inconsistent mixture as he progresses 'from philosophy to poetry and religion' (according to the commitment of 1796) to synthesize the two into a new mythology where the tragic plays a pivotal role by supplying the 'form of reason' (115): the tragic represents ethics, or, more concretely, it assimilates what is left out of neo-classical art once aesthetics identifies beauty as an inherent quality.

Georg Wilhelm Hegel (1807)

Opposition is the possibility of unification, and the extent to which in affliction life is felt as an opposite is also the extent of the possibility of resuming it again. It is in the fact that even the enemy is felt as life that there lies the possibility of reconciling fate. This reconciliation is thus neither the destruction or subjugation of something alien, nor a contradiction between consciousness of one's self and the hoped-for difference in another's idea of one's self, nor a contradiction between desert in the eyes of the law and the actualization of the same, or between man as concept and man as reality. This sensing of life, a sensing which finds itself again, is love, and in love fate is reconciled.

Hegel 1948: 232

In the tragic views of Schiller and Schelling, outside forces (objective necessity) threatening man (subjective freedom) with annihilation were represented by fate. The same idea appears in the reflections on the tragic hero in Hölderlin's 'The "Ground" for *Empedocles*'. At the same time, in the 'Remarks on *Antigone*' (1803), Hölderlin notes that 'it is the main tendency in the mode of representation of our time to designate something, to possess a skill, since the lack of destiny, the *dysmoron*, is our deficiency' (Hölderlin 1988: 113-14). G.W.F. Hegel (1770-1831), his close friend, also begins to feel that the Moderns lack destiny and to search for a new heroism. Writing in the mid-1790s as a critic of the Church he reflects on the place of religion in the modern world, especially in a post-oligarchic, republican nation-state, hoping 'to contribute to the spread of the Kantian spirit of freedom by way of theological enlightenment. He thus attempts to think through the possible establishment of a public religion, which – unlike the existing one – would be a truly civic religion, promoting rather than suppressing reason and freedom' (Henrich 1997: 128). By 1797-9 these reflections acquire a tragic framework as freedom is no longer the overcoming of necessity but rather the unification of opposites. In presenting reason as an antinomian force which has to enter into conflict with itself and at the same time can overcome its inner discord because it recognizes it, the socio-political analyst comes into a position to criticize Kant and Fichte, and establish his philosophical vocation.

In the Frankfurt essay known as 'The Spirit of Christianity and its Fate' (1798-9), Hegel seeks a religious solution to modern alienation, to man's separation from God and state. In an age of fragmentation and individualism, man lacks a destiny that would drive him to self-realization. 'It is to *moira*, with its dynamic impersonality but existential immanence, that Hegel seems to attach the paradoxical but decisive category of "fated guilt", of an order of culpability in and through which an individual (the tragic hero) comes wholly into his own – comes home *fatally* to himself without relinquishing ... his at-oneness with life' (Steiner 1984: 24). However, Hegel takes Schelling's notion of the unavoidable crime and places it within the hero, turning ethical nature itself into something tragic. Schelling's *fatum* is no longer a power of the objective world. It is a moment in the development of consciousness. In the inner development of identity, destiny is the stage of self-division within ethical nature since it represents consciousness of oneself as something hostile. Conflict is internalized. In destiny, ethics faces the law in the court that it itself established. 'By "destiny", Hegel thus understands this capacity which an individual or a people has to live its separation or its sundering as its own, and that is to say as this tragedy which it has to assume as its own. For this people or this individual – tragic consciousness – life is what separates itself in itself' (Beistegui 2000: 16). While using in early texts like this one the word *Schicksal* for both fate and destiny, Hegel will soon introduce a terminological distinction

between Fate (*Schicksal, Fatum*) and Destiny (*Bestimmung*). In addition, he makes frequent use of 'necessity' (*Notwendigkeit*) as a transitional category: that is, he attempts to demonstrate how it is transformed from something 'blind' into something that is rational and self-aware. Hegel speaks of Fate, more often than not, as something blind, something that possesses no conscious necessity for us. ... Over against this Hegel posits Destiny, the realm of spirit, which is a realm of dawning self-consciousness, that philosophical point of view which recognizes the spiritual *necessity* of all that really is.

Ruprecht 1994: 80-1

While Fate may be a matter of blind necessity, Destiny acknowledges human responsibility and courage.

Hegel cannot agree with those who, like Hölderlin, considered Kant the 'Moses' of the German nation and praised him for bringing 'the rigorous law from the sacred mountain' (Hölderlin 1988: 137). He conducts a critique of Kantian and Fichtean philosophy through a historico-theological inquiry: the confrontation between Judaism and Christianity, which he mediates through Greek fate. Specifically, he attacks moral formalism through a critique of Judaism as a rigid dualism – an irreconcilable opposition between the human and the divine, life and law, the individual and the universal. After comparing the tragic consciousness of the Jewish and the Greek people, he proposes that the sundered forces may have been reconciled in Christianity which opposed love to law and bridged the gap between man and God through Jesus' incarnation. True destiny arrives with Christianity, and so does the dialectic, Hegel implies. Thus the origins of his philosophical method lie in a comparison between Judaism and Christianity where the tragic division of the ethical world is healed in love.

However, in the same essay Hegel discovers that Christian reconciliation too fails because it cannot contain life as differentiated unity of the divine and the actual, spirit and reality. Christianity too is self-divided, and therefore subject to fate. Love may redeem law but cannot overcome tragic destiny. The essay concludes:

Between these extremes of the multiple or diminished consciousness of friendship, hate, or indifference toward the world, between these extremes which occur within the opposition between God and the world, between the divine and life, the Christian church has oscillated to and fro, but it is contrary to its essential character to find peace in a nonpersonal living beauty. And it is its fate that church and state, worship and life, piety and virtue, spiritual and worldly action, can never dissolve into one.

Hegel 1948: 301

50

Since Christianity too is tragically divided, reconciliation must be sought in life itself, specifically, in a consciousness which embraces and affirms life as destiny. The Idealist dialectic, which Hegel first identifies here in the Christian spirit (before proposing it as the foundation of all ethics), is the tragic process of self-division in fate, reconciliation in love and affirmation in ethics. Thus the tragedy of history and the tragedy of self-consciousness merge.

If reconciliation on the basis of religion alone is today impossible, it should be sought in the ethico-political realm. Pursuing his critique of formalist *Moralität*, Hegel turns to the ethical totality, trying to found a new moral philosophy. He develops his theory of the tragic as a dialectical model in the Jena essay 'On the Scientific Ways of Treating Natural Law' (1802-3), where the dramaturgical approach serves a study in modern political culture. He resolves the Kantian/Fichtean opposition between universal and particular, law and individuality, by positing an absolute idea of *Sittlichkeit*/ethical life that contains within itself in a dynamic identity the 'state of nature' and the 'state of law'. This destinal force keeps the two powers of inorganic law and living individuality (Hölderlin's aorgic and organic) in a conflict that is perpetually activated, negated and transcended. Hegel illustrates this with the conclusion of Aeschylus' *Oresteia*, namely, the conflict between Apollo and the Eumenides before the 'ethical organization, the people of Athens', which ends with the reconciliation brought about by Athena. This is the tragic process of self-division and self-reconciliation 'which the absolute eternally performs with itself: that it eternally gives birth to itself into objectivity, and in this its form it hereby gives itself over to suffering and death, and raises itself up out of its ashes into magnificence' (quoted in Adler 1983: 220). Thus it is the universal itself which particularizes itself and which, in this movement of self-opposition, posits itself as destiny and reconciles itself with itself. What Hölderlin wrote about the 'whole' in 'On the Difference of Poetic Modes' and Schelling about tragedy find here their historical fulfilment. In Hegel's drama of the absolute, 'the tragic and the dialectic coincide' (Szondi 2002: 16). The tragic is the form *and* the movement of the dialectical, the way it occurs in reality. 'The tragedy of ethics is nothing other than the ethical manifestation of the tragedy which the absolute itself is, and which fulfils itself only in the tragic completion of ethical totality. The being of the absolute is nothing other than the tragedy of its manifestation, and the originality of the Hegelian conception of the tragic is to conceive of it as the content of speculative philosophy' (Beistegui 2000: 19). In the essay, the tragic finds its philosophical content and reconciles all Idealist oppositions in a grandiose catharsis of passion and redemption. At the end of the eighteenth century, Hegel is reaching an epoch-making conclusion: if conflict is universal fate, then dialectic is the painful and glorious human destiny.

August Schlegel (1809)

When ... we contemplate the relations of our existence to the extreme limit of possibilities: when we reflect on its entire dependence on a chain of causes and effects, stretching beyond our ken: when we consider how weak and helpless, and doomed to struggle against the enormous powers of nature, and conflicting appetites, we are cast on the shores of an unknown world, as it were, shipwrecked at our very birth; how we are subject to all kinds of errors and deceptions, any one of which may be our ruin; that in our passions we cherish an enemy in our bosoms; how every moment demands from us, in the name of the most sacred duties, the sacrifice of our dearest inclinations, and how at one blow we may be robbed of all that we have acquired with much toil and difficulty; ... when we think upon all this, every heart which is not dead to feeling must be overpowered by an inexpressible melancholy, for which there is no other counterpoise than the consciousness of a vocation transcending the limits of this earthly life. This is the tragic tone of mind.

August Schlegel, *Lectures on Dramatic Art and Literature*, quoted in Dukore 1974: 500

According to the tragic paradox of human action, first formulated by Schiller and subsequently elaborated by Schelling and Hölderlin, freedom reaches self-awareness when it resists nature's attack. In the third of his *Lectures on Dramatic Art and Literature* (delivered in 1808-9 and published in 1809-11), before examining tragic poetry, Schlegel defines the tragic along comparable lines. He sees inner liberty and external necessity as the two poles of the tragic world whose conflict brings them into full manifestation: invisible spiritual powers can become visible and recognizable only through their clash with external forces capable of being appreciated by the senses. Thus moral freedom can be displayed only through its collision with natural impulses. Tragedy presents repugnant subjects and triggers

53

overwhelming sorrows in order to acknowledge objective necessity and assert freedom. With its organic, mysterious unity of action (which mechanistic Neo-classical reason could never capture), it helps its audience overcome the melancholy of the shipwrecked life and the tragic tone of mind. To the Romantics, unity is not classic but unique, bound to the specificity of time, place, language, genre and the like. Each individual creation invents and embodies its own rules according to the principles of self-legislating autonomy. In dramatizing this tragic freedom, more than timeless, art is true.

Arthur Schopenhauer (1818)

[T]he end of this highest poetical achievement [that is, tragedy] is the representation of the terrible side of life. The unspeakable pain, the wail of humanity, the triumph of evil, the scornful mastery of chance, and the irretrievable fall of the just and innocent, is here presented to us; and in this lies a significant hint of the nature of the world and of existence. It is the strife of will with itself, which here, completely unfolded at the highest grade of its objectivity, comes into full prominence.

Schopenhauer, *The World as Will and Idea*,
quoted in Dukore 1974: 516

In his book *The World as Will and Idea* (1818), Arthur Schopenhauer (1788-1860) proposes that, by depicting great misfortune and unjust suffering, tragedy reveals the terrible spectacle of life, the tragic condition of humanity – the antagonism of the voracious will against itself. This antagonism becomes visible in the suffering of mankind. What others call fate is but insidious chance and error. The tragic consists in the process of the objectification of the will from blind urge to self-knowledge to self-destruction. It does not represent any revolt but mere individuation, the separation of person from the totality of life. The demand for poetic justice is based on a misconception of not just tragedy but the world itself. There is no moral beauty. The tragic unfolds the terrible spectacle of life – the pain of the innocents, the fall of the just, the triumph of the evil. Existence is sin, life is fall, horror is the normal state of affairs, and 'eternal justice' finds fault with the individuated self. The only appropriate response to the tragedy of life is resignation to fate, 'the surrender not merely of life but of the very will to live'. The Romantic ideal of heroic transgression is hollow, freedom is meaningless. Necessity always wins. The hero atones not for his individual sin but for original sin itself, the crime of existence. Hegel's historical-ethical account is rejected as man, who no longer feels at home in history, takes leave of a world of struggle.

Art helps us escape from the necessary suffering of self-conscious life, and leads us to perfect resignation, abolishing all willing and giving up salvation. 'Tragedy, in Schopenhauer's view, is an especially valuable art form because, in addition to nourishing the aesthetic attitude, as do all forms of art, it reminds us, by its content, of the many motives we have for turning toward art, and away from the will. It is thus peculiarly self-reinforcing. For tragedy represents (in a general form, fit for contemplation) all the sufferings to which human beings are prone if they live the life of will and desire' (Nussbaum 1991: 90). Pleasure in tragedy comes not from the beautiful but from the most intense sublime, the fact that in the presence of catastrophe we are disenchanted with the world and turn away from the will to live. 'This is Schopenhauer's own version of the dialectic of pity and fear, intimacy and alienness, as we are drawn to a suffering which we acknowledge as our own, while through the framing, tranquillizing power of the aesthetic, we distance ourselves derisively from the whole grotesquely pointless spectacle' (Eagleton 2003: 173). In this context, freedom means unreflective detachment. Instead of helping us overcome the tragic tone of mind, as Schlegel argued, tragedy convinces us that life is a bad dream from which we must awake. As Schopenhauer put it epigrammatically, 'tragedy so ends that nothing can come after' (Dukore 1974: 522). Modern tragedy of destiny (*Schicksalstragödie*) is superior to its ancient counterpart because its protagonists consciously embrace their destiny. The quest for justice is thus abandoned. Suffering is meaningful to the extent that it teaches the tragic spirit of resignation. Faced with the aspect of the world that fights our will, we feel tempted to renounce our will, to no longer will it. Knowledge derived from the will, instead of serving it, turns against it.

Victor Hugo (1827)

To hastily summarize the facts we have thus far noted, poetry
has three ages, each corresponding to an epoch in society: The
ode, the epic, the drama. Primitive periods are lyrical, ancient
times are epic, modern times are dramatic. The ode sings of
eternity, the epic solemnizes history, the *drame* paints life. The
characteristic of the first type of poetry is naiveté; the characteristic of the second is simplicity; the characteristic of the third
is faithfulness to life. The rhapsodists mark the transition from
lyric to epic poets, as do the romancers from epic to dramatic
poets. Historians are born with the second epoch; chroniclers
and critics with the third. ... The ode takes life from the ideal,
the epic from the grandiose, the *drame* from the real. Lastly,
this threefold poetry flows from great sources: the Bible,
Homer, and Shakespeare.

Hugo, Preface to *Cromwell*, quoted in Gerould 2000: 305

The centre for literary theory has moved from Italy in the sixteenth
century, to France in the seventeenth century, to Germany near the
end of the eighteenth and beyond. Given the prominence of tragic
theory in Germany, it is interesting to see what is happening in the
two earlier centres of criticism during the same period. Throughout
the eighteenth century and well into the nineteenth, Italian theory
continues to focus on the composition of tragedies, discussing questions of technique (such as the three unities), style (such as
decorum), rhetoric (such as appropriate language), thematics (such
as subject matter), moral teaching, and more recently, Classicism vs
Romanticism. The question of tragedy is a genre issue, namely, what
is the true nature of this literary form. Even when Italians like
Alessandro Manzoni (1785-1873) read German theorists such as the
Schlegels, they draw structural, rather than metaphysical lessons.

Similar trends prevail in France. In *On Germany* (1810), Madame
de Staël (1766-1817) compares French (southern Classical) and

57

German (northern Romantic) theatre on the basis of their distinct national characteristics, adding also comments on Shakespeare. In *Racine and Shakespeare* (1823 and 1825), Stendhal (1783-1842) surveys (again in the context of a Classicism vs Romanticism comparison) dramatic illusion and other elements of tragedy that please a contemporary audience, rejecting the demand for the unities. In the preface to his *Cromwell* (1827), quoted above, Victor Hugo (1802-85) discusses rules that writers should follow as well as the relation of drama to reality, historical or modern. Benjamin Constant (1767-1830), translating Schiller in 1809, and Alfred de Vigny (1797-1863), translating Shakespeare in 1829, write on adapting foreign tragedies to French conventions and standards. These authors continue the robust tradition, dating back to the age of Corneille and Racine, of writing critical prefaces for their plays and translations, a practice that did not take root in Germany despite exceptions like Hebbel.

Constant in 1829 and Alfred de Musset (1810-57) in 1838 consider the most appropriate basis for contemporary tragedy. The former writer (together with Bentham, the most influential liberal of his era) rejects French Neo-classical 'tragedy of passion' and German Romantic 'tragedy of character' in favour of a future 'tragedy of society' portraying individuals in moral conflict with the world, caught among social relations, laws and institutions, which constitute fate for the Moderns: 'The social order, the action of society on the individual, in diverse phases and in diverse epochs, this network of institutions and conventions, which envelops us from our birth and is not broken until our death, these are the tragic motivations which one [playwright] needs to know how to manipulate. They are entirely equal to the fatality of the ancients; their weight composes all that was invincible and oppressive in that fatality' (Constant 1983: 107). Musset, after surveying the genre with particular emphasis on the French Baroque, recommends subjects from national history, a recommendation also made during the same period by the German Georg Gottfried Gervinus in his monumental *History of the German National Poetic Literature* (1835-42).

It has been argued that, when regarding post-Enlightenment tragedy, from the mid eighteenth century onwards, the Protestant component occupies virtually the entire stage.

58

Romance tragedy disappears, and Germany holds for over a century – Lessing, Schiller, Hölderlin, Kleist, Büchner, Hebbel, Wagner, Hauptmann … – a veritable monopoly of tragic invention. … From the eighteenth to the twentieth century, tragedy is thus the dominant form in the only northern culture which hasn't yet achieved its national unity. … In the absence of a stable political structure, and of the atmosphere of compromise which usually follows from it, all political values and anti-values of modern Europe achieve in Germany a metaphysical purity which makes their representation *sub specie tragica* almost ineluctable.

Moretti 1994: 99

Considering French and English trends, though, it might be more accurate to place this development in the third decade of the nineteenth century, when the generation of Vigny, Balzac, Hugo, and Musset (and Dumas père and Sand) concludes that, judging from the failures of Goethe, Hölderlin, Shelley, Wordsworth and many others in the composition of tragedy, the moment of this rare genre has passed. As Shelley put it in 1821: 'In periods of the decay of social life, the drama sympathises with that decay. Tragedy becomes a cold imitation of the form of the great masterpieces of antiquity, divested of all harmonious accompaniment of the kindred arts; and often the very form misunderstood, or a weak attempt to teach certain doctrines, which the writer considers as moral truths' (Shelley 1909: 136). The legendary past has been conquered by the historical romances of Sir Walter Scott (1771-1832). Honoré de Balzac (1799-1850), like Stendhal before him, gives up early the idea of becoming a dramatist after he determines that, if the times demand a theatre of truth, the novel of social relevance can provide that perspective much better. Most critics and playwrights turn their attention to the new genre of the *drame* whose moral purpose superseded dramatic laws and whose popularity defied critical respect. Eugène Scribe (1791-1861) is the first playwright who does not write any prefaces to his plays, confident that they are so well made, they need no supporting general argument. The need for theory has ceased as, with the triumph of Romanticism in the 1820s, romantic theatre collapses and tragedy comes to an end.

In the Preface to *Cromwell*, Hugo concludes his dialectical interpretation of literary history by saying that 'society begins by singing
its dreams, then narrates its deeds, and finally sets about describing
what it thinks' (306). The 1840s in Europe, which opened with
Schelling's return to the campus amphitheatre in 1841 and closed
with *The Communist Manifesto* in 1848, will prove him right but in
a different sense: society's thinking during the subsequent era takes
place away from both the theatre and tragic theory. Structures of
tragic conflict will surface next in the historical views of Karl Marx
and Alexis de Tocqueville (White 1973: 194-5, 204-18, 286-7, 328-30).
As Goethe, Hegel, Schleiermacher, Coleridge, Bentham, Walter Scott,
Leopardi, Pushkin and other towering figures pass away during the
1830s, while others cease to write or take increasingly conservative
positions, much will depend on struggles over both the Hegelian
legacy and the future of history.

Thomas de Quincey (1840)

Shakespeare's tragic life is our own life exalted and selected:
the Greek tragic life presupposed another life, the spectator's,
thrown into relief before it.

de Quincey 1890: 347

In his essay 'Theory of Greek Tragedy' (1840), Thomas de Quincey
(1785-1859) treats Greek tragedy as a 'dark problem' not because of its
meaning but on account of its differences from modern tragedy. He
argues that the tragic muses of Greece and England stand so far aloof
that they hardly recognize each other. The philosophical nature of
their distance can be described by the device of the play within a play
in Baroque English and Spanish drama. In an introvoluting series,
each stage/term is a mode of non-reality to the previous exterior
stage/term of the series. Thus what the inner life of the mimetic play
in *Hamlet* is to Hamlet's outer life, Greek tragedy is to the outer
tragedy of England: they both presuppose the spectator's life thrown
into relief as exterior stage before it. While Shakespeare's tragic life
reflects our own, ancient tragic life was never that of the Greeks. A
'gulf of shadows' separated those spectators from the phantasmagoria.

The ancient idealized life operates within the modern ordinary life
of the spectator. It possesses no development, struggle or conflict. It
uses the derivative elevating power of fate as opposed to a direct
moral one. It presents only fixed situations of indefinite suffering,
sublime states of monotonous gloom and grand attitudes of enduring
remotion. Its retrospective movement manifests its overall retroces-
sive character. However, we can observe the same manifestation in
the relation between Greek and English tragedy. The ancient 'intro-
volution' (de Quincey's neologism), this life within life which is out
of all proportion to the realities of the spectator, also depicts the
modern situation and its place in the *theatrum mundi*: like Hamlet,
Hamlet needs another tragedy, a Greek one, to make sense of its
tragic condition. Greek tragedy can hardly be more different, and yet

more relevant to the one in which Hamlet is starring. In this sense, history is a state of retrocession as each drama may postulate faithfully the intense life of its time but becomes real by staging another drama, each era assuming the functions of real life in its relation to the next interior play of the series. In life's *theatrum mundi*, each original situation is a mimic, an unreal state which becomes real life with respect to the secondary state, that is, by viewing such a state as a stage, one 'treated upon a scale so sensibly different from the proper life of the spectator as to impress him profoundly with the feeling of its idealization' (347). The tragic idea here is that there is no sense of real life without the experience of the stage, and no modern life without the staging of the Greeks. The world is not a stage, but it presupposes one.

Søren Kierkegaard (1843)

Our age has lost all the substantial categories of family, state, and race. It must leave the individual entirely to himself, so that in a stricter sense he becomes his own creator, his guilt is consequently sin, his pain remorse; but this nullifies the tragic. Also, that which in a stricter sense is to be called the tragedy of suffering has really lost its tragic interest, for the power from which the suffering comes has lost its significance, and the spectators cry: 'Heaven helps those who help themselves!'

Kierkegaard 1959: 147

Hegel's synthesis of faith and reason, philosophy and religion, church and state breaks up around 1840. A process which started less than a year after the master's death in 1831 has run its course by the end of the decade. When Schelling is brought by the King back to the active academic life in order to teach at the University of Berlin in 1841, it is too late even for him to destroy the 'dragon seed of Hegelianism' and redeem the original promise of Idealism. Among the hundreds of intellectuals attending with deep disappointment his notorious lectures on revelation and Christianity are figures like Mikhail Bakunin, Jacob Burckhardt, Johann Droysen, Friedrich Engels, Ludwig Feuerbach (who has just published *The Essence of Christianity*), Ferdinand Lassalle, Leopold von Ranke, Friedrich Carl von Savigny and the young Kierkegaard, who months earlier that year defended his Master's thesis and left Copenhagen after breaking his year-old engagement with Regine Olsen. Søren Kierkegaard (1813-55) responds to the exhaustion of Idealism and the emergence of Left Hegelianism with a post-literary configuration, building during the 1840s a literary career on the pseudonymous mock treatise. This project enables him to turn his disaffection with official Lutheranism into an ironic study of modernity from the standpoint of artistic pietism.

Kierkegaard's first major work, *Either/Or* (1843), shows how the modern inability to follow either an aesthetic or an ethical way leads to despair over the very possibility of fashioning one's own life. The book comprises, in two main sections, a collection of papers by a fictional author 'A', followed by the responses of author 'B', each representing two contrasting ways of life. The third piece in the book 'The Ancient Tragical Motif as Reflected in the Modern' brings to a close the first period of tragic theory inaugurated by Schiller half a century earlier. Kierkegaard draws a distinction between tragedy and the tragic, arguing that through the ages the concept of the tragic (the essence of tragedy) remains the same (Kierkegaard 1959: 137) but its conception has changed. His goal is to define how the tragic has been embodied in modern tragedy so that its true nature will come to light. The modern conception of tragedy differs from the ancient one in respect to three Aristotelian categories: agency, guilt and compassion. Central in each case is the notion that 'the ancient world did not have subjectivity fully self-conscious and reflective. Even if the individual moved freely, he still rested in the substantial categories of state, family, and destiny' (141).

Regarding agency first, it has been known since Aristotle that in tragedy 'individuals do not act in order to present characters, but the characters are included for the sake of the action. ... The peculiarity of ancient tragedy is that the action does not issue exclusively from the character, that the action does not find its sufficient explanation in subjective reflection and decision, but that the action has a relative admixture of suffering [passion, *passio*]' (140-1). Thought and character are the source of action, yet character is not entirely sufficient. The action is therefore infused with its own suffering, supplemented by the chorus and the monologue. In modern tragedy, however, action derives sufficiently from the exhaustive reflection within dialogue. Here 'situation and character are really predominant. The tragic hero, conscious of himself as a subject, is fully reflective, and this reflection has not only reflected him out of every immediate relation to state, race, and destiny, but it has often reflected him out of his own preceding life. ... The hero stands and falls entirely on his own acts' (141). Therefore in modern tragedy situation and conscious character are central while action and suffering are less important.

Regarding guilt next, 'just as the action in Greek tragedy is intermediate between activity and passivity (action and suffering), so is also the hero's guilt, and therein lies the tragic collision. On the other hand, the more the subjectivity becomes reflected, the more one sees the individual left to himself, ... all the more does his guilt become ethical. Between these two extremes lies the tragic' (142). The two extremes are the purely aesthetic, represented by the mixed nature of the ancient (guilt balanced between action and suffering), and the purely ethical, represented by modern self-reflectivity. The inherent ambiguity of being and yet not being responsible makes ancient guilt aesthetic while the unambiguous grounding in personal responsibility makes modern guilt ethical. The inwardness of modern responsibility transforms the hero's aesthetic guilt into an ethical one and makes him into an evil person who cannot generate enough aesthetic interest.

Last, as regards compassion (Aristotelian pity), the revelation of the two kinds of tragic guilt generates two corresponding kinds of sympathetic response: tragic sorrow (the experience of forces outside one's control) and tragic pain (an individual's self-inflicted suffering). 'In ancient tragedy the sorrow is deeper, the pain less; in modern, the pain greater, the sorrow less. Sorrow always contains something more substantial than pain. Pain always implies a reflection over suffering which sorrow does not know' (145-6). In ancient tragedy, the sorrow is deeper because guilt is charged with aesthetic ambiguity. In modern tragedy, where the pain is greater, 'the bitterest pain is manifestly remorse, but remorse has ethical not aesthetic reality. It is the bitterest pain because it has the total transparency of guilt, but just because of this transparency it does not interest us aesthetically' (146). Whereas the true tragic dialectic requires the categories of guilt and innocence, of transparent sorrow and obscure pain (149), in modern times ancient sorrow has given way to remorse and greater pain owing to a transmutation of the aesthetic tragic into the ethical which in turn nullifies the tragic. This accounts for the centrality of remorse in Romantic drama from Coleridgean tragedy to Wagnerian opera (Steiner 1963: 129-33).

Thus in all three categories, there is a transition from the ancient aesthetic to the modern ethical. The interiorization of subjectivity into reflectivity radicalizes responsibility and transforms ambiguity into self-consciousness. The ancient tragic categories are characterized by remarkable equivocality: in agency, action is an admixture of decision and event, deed and circumstance; guilt mixes activity and passivity, ignorance and heritage; and in response, deep sorrow comes out of the mixture of innocence and responsibility. In contrast, the modern tragic cannot tolerate aesthetic ambiguity, forcing individuals into self-conscious ethical choices.

The second part of the essay begins with an address to the gathering of the secret society of the Fellowship of the Dead/*Symparanekromenoi* (Kierkegaard 1959: 149-50), continues with a digression on the fragmentary nature of all human endeavours, especially artistic ones, and culminates in the transposition of an ancient tragic motif into the modern tonality, namely, the composition of Kierkegaard's own *Antigone*. At the end of the philosophical examination of the conception of the tragic as it appears in the ancient and the modern motifs, and as the author addresses himself directly to his Fellow Moribunds, the reader is suddenly reminded that this disquisition has been an address before an audience. Kierkegaard the 'dramatist' (Emanuel Hirsch) has staged (as he will repeatedly in the future) an occasion for a literary masque whereby the paper on the tragic by aestheticist A has been read before the society and edited by Victor Eremita. The modern tragic concept finds dramatic expression in this piece of mixed genre and theatrical flair. In his dissertation, Adorno identifies in Kierkegaard's work many elements of the literary baroque as defined by Walter Benjamin, such as inwardness, disguise, seduction, pomposity, cruelty, martyrdom, allegory, and in general what he calls the 'dialectic of melancholy' (Adorno 1989: 62). Any reflection on the possibility of tragedy is bound to enact the drama of dialectics in the same way that the loss of ancient aesthetics constitutes the tragedy of modern ethics.

Throughout his life, Kierkegaard has a strong interest in the present condition of literature and art in general. In Mann's *Doctor Faustus*, the Devil (who interrupts Adrian Leverkühn's reading of another essay in Kierkegaard's *Either/Or*, namely A's study of Mozart's *Don Giovanni*) calls Kierkegaard 'the Christian in love with aesthetics' (Mann 1968: 235). The tragic ancient world is fraught with ambiguity, contradiction and undecidability while the tragic modern one is haunted by isolation, reflection and anxiety. The proper response to the latter world is 'an artistic heritage' (Kierkegaard 1959:

151) of calculated transitoriness, programmatic incompletion, and indolent desultoriness. If art is condemned to belatedness, it can thematize its predicament by staging fragmentariness: 'Let us then describe our purpose as an attempt in fragmentary pursuits, or in the art of writing posthumous papers. ... the art consists in producing an enjoyment which never actually becomes present, but always has an element of the past in it, so that it is present in the past' (150). This advocacy of 'the fragmentary imperative' (Schulte-Sasse 1997: 287-358) is mocking poetry's cult of ruins (incompletion and the accidental) and of personality (the poet's flight of thought). Kierkegaard's advocacy has in mind Friedrich Schlegel, the master ironist and theoretician of the Romantic fragment. Giving his own twist to Fichte's self-positing I, Schlegel came up with the view that the essence of self-consciousness is captured by the authentic contradiction of irony, the unavoidable combination of total commitment and reflective detachment. 'The concept of Romantic irony converges with the concept of criticism, just as it does with the concept of reflection. All three aim at overcoming the classical aesthetic of representation with an aesthetic of production, in which what is to be produced is not so much a work as an ability or an attitude that can induce a more humane praxis' (Schulte-Sasse 1988: 154). Kierkegaard attacked that view savagely for its amoral self-absorption in the section 'Irony after Fichte' of his 1841 dissertation *The Concept of Irony, with Constant Reference to Socrates* (Kierkegaard 1965: 302-16).

The ancient Antigone inherits the sins of her father and suffers in part because her destiny is to experience the wrath of the gods for his guilt. Thus her defiance of Creon's edict is not a destiny chosen independently but resonates with Oedipus's fateful destiny: her family's fate directly affects hers. Her tragic guilt inheres in the ambiguity of her innocence when she acts as an individual and as a sister. Kierkegaard improvises for his own Antigone what Kenneth Burke might call a 'psychology' (Burke 1969: 246). His melancholic heroine is driven by the modern ethical guilt rather than the ancient aesthetic one, as she is fully conscious of her situation. Here there is no external conflict, no wrath of gods causing the destruction of an entire house but only an internal conflict in the reflective world of the heroine. Her father died without his fault coming to light. She is the only one who knows of Oedipus's transgression, and by keeping it secret out of filial piety, she protects her father's honour and her family's name. Unfolding inwardly, this exclusively personal responsibility causes anxiety, which Kierkegaard considers 'a truly tragic category ... determined by reflection' (Kierkegaard 1959: 153). Anxiety constitutes the subject's interiorization of, and preoccupation with, sorrow, and involves a reflection upon past or future time. Up to this point, this Antigone is not tragic but rather demonstrates qualities associated with the predicament of modern isolation. In order to establish a tragic collision in his tragedy, Kierkegaard introduces the force of love: while Antigone honours her father's memory by keeping his secret, her love for a young man requires that she share her secret with him. It is this passionate collision that will lead her to her end since 'the memory of her father is the cause of her death; ... her unhappy love makes that memory kill her' (162).

Kierkegaard accepts that, when homogeneous forces clash, they produce a profound tragic collision: 'The more sympathetic the colliding forces are, the deeper but also the more homogeneous they are, the more important the collision' (160). In ancient tragedy, a collision occurs between Antigone's action (the brother's burial) and her passivity (the necessary suffering on account of her membership in a fated family). In modern tragedy, collision is internal to her being because of the necessary isolation-through-reflection dictated by her era. Destruction occurs not through suffering in the hands of wrathful deity but because the heroine reflects herself out of continuity with a community (family, destiny or state) and into a state of pathetic isolation. Having criticized the ancient tragic for aesthetic ambiguity and the modern one for ethical egocentrism, Kierkegaard proposes a literary alternative by re-writing/repeating the *Antigone*: he composes a spiritual tragedy in prose as a posthumous Romantic parable. Since his Antigone, because of love, is caught in a tragic collision, she is no longer modern (nor religious yet) but something else, 'wholly spiritual' (160). As a result, the tragic is partially eradicated because reflective agency and conscious pain take precedence over public action and non-reflective suffering. There is no action, no outward movement, and no performance in this drama. Like the members of the *Symparanekromenoi* and like A, the author of this posthumously edited essay, the maiden of this parable, although living, 'is in another sense dead' (155).

During one of the most self-consciously historical decades of the last several centuries, Kierkegaard rejects historicism, ignores politics, scorns theology and responds to an individual calling – that of becoming a modern individual, one left entirely to himself.

Kierkegaard's project is the precise antithesis of the Kantian thesis and the Hegelian synthesis. Against Kant, he pursues the plan of concrete ontology; against Hegel, he pursues the plan of an ontology that does not succumb to the existent by absorbing it into itself. He therefore revises the process of post-Kantian idealism: he surrenders the claim of identity. ... Along with Hegelian identity, he sacrifices the Kantian transcendental objectivity. ... The individual becomes, for Kierkegaard, the bearer of a material meaning that the philosophy of identity was unable to realize in contingent sensuous material, whereas the abstract Kantian 'I think' did not suffice to confirm the existence it had mastered as meaningful. Hegel is turned inside out: world history is for Hegel what the individual is for Kierkegaard.

Adorno 1989: 74

Due to the loss of ancient bonds and the ensuing isolation with its secretive pursuits, modern existence suffers from melancholy and despair, giving the age its strong tendency in the direction of the comic since each isolated individual asserts his subjectivity as mere form and 'his own accidental individuality over against necessary development' (Kierkegaard 1959: 140). Thus in reality the only available form of the tragic in modernity is the comic. On this basis, Kierkegaard pursues a radically ethical vocation by embracing the aesthetic autonomy of authorship with the despair of comical inwardness. His despair, like Heine's pursuit of irony and Marx's interest in farce, resonates with Hegel's remark that, as the individuals of bourgeois society succeeded the heroes of the aristocratic era, comedy followed tragedy in the theatre of the world. It also finds an uncanny parallel in de Quincey's idea of the modern mimic.

Friedrich Hebbel (1844)

[D]ramatic art is intended to help complete the world-historical process which is taking place in our times and which aims not to overthrow the existing institutions – political, religious, and moral – of the human race but to give them a deeper foundation, thus actually securing them against revolution.

Hebbel, Preface to Mary Magdalene, quoted in Brandt
1998: 74

Post-idealist writers agree with Hegel that the tragic involves a conflict of incompatible ethical claims but they discover this conflict not in Hegel's ethical world of the citizens' community but in the alienating process which leads from the original nexus of being to the individuation of becoming. In this view, conflict becomes self-division, and its hero is a tragic personality (rather than character) enduring and defying a cruel fate as it is being destroyed by clashing responsibilities. This psychological approach turns tragic action from a public to a private event, from an opposition of moral laws to a confusion of feelings pulled by personal dilemmas. Life is tragic since a person is at war with fate (world-will) where every moral choice entails opposition to the world. In such a war, there is no resolution, no historical justification, only existential indignation and metaphysical revolt. Tragic vision becomes demonic in its espousal of radical pessimism.

The German playwright Friedrich Hebbel (1813-63) receives his doctorate the same year as Kierkegaard, with a long essay called *My Word on the Drama*. In it, he rejects Hegelian reconciliation and, like Kierkegaard, defines existence as tragic on the basis of the unresolvable struggle between individuality and general order: the working of the will towards individuation disrupts the equilibrium of fate and produces personal expression at the cost of guilt and doom. Already in this essay, Hebbel's intense interest in processes of change is paramount. So is the psychological and metaphysical nature of this interest which will focus on mythical and historical topics, strip them of their political and institutional dimension, and highlight the tragic predicament of 'isolated', uncompromising individuals caught in universal conflicts with society, state, faith, gender and other forms of totality.

A year later, in the preface to his third play, *Mary Magdalene* (1844), a 'tragedy of common life', Hebbel understands tragedy as the historiography of crisis. So far, the highest drama has manifested itself in two historical moments of extreme crisis – the subordination of the individual to fate in antiquity (reflected in its tragedy) and the emancipation of the individual in the Reformation (reflected in Shakespeare). Since Goethe, drama has been grappling with the depiction of a third crisis, one involving the individual and his institutions which have grown contradictory. The great heritage of the present age is the dissonances arising from this transitional condition. They may generate fluctuations and divisions in private and public lives but, contrary to accusations, these dissonances do not demand new and unprecedented institutions but only 'a better foundation for the existing ones so that they rest on nothing other than morality and necessity, which are the same thing, and thus exchange the external fixed point whereby they have hitherto been partially secured for an inner centre of gravity from which they can be derived entirely' (Brandt 1998: 73).

This is the world-historical process presently unfolding, and drama is called upon to contribute to the desired conclusion, producing 'the new form of humanity in which everything will once again find its place' (73), overcoming fragmentation and rediscovering life's lost unity. To Hebbel's mind, even though bourgeois tragedy has fallen out of favour, for this mission it remains preferable to heroic tragedy because in the former the circle of the tragic form is completed when we see a universally human fate and a wholly inevitable outcome – a necessary act with world-historical purpose destroying the individual who attempts in vain to carry it out in an ethically consistent way. Furthermore, such a genuine representation depicting the process of spirit as historical development makes the question of whether a drama gets staged superfluous. As in social life, so in the theatre: internal arrangement, rather than external fate, determines its value.

The Tragic Idea

At a time of historical crisis which threatens to burst into a revolution, the goal of bourgeois tragedy (which constitutes the drama of social criticism) is to help provide modern unstable institutions with stronger foundations so that they can continue to rest on the inner centre of self-control, namely, morality and necessity, which excludes from world process the perilous operations of freedom. Life development means that humans work towards their destruction. Contrary to what the early Romantics thought, the tragic does not consist in the struggle of freedom against fate but in the very acquisition of fate. Freedom means violation of limits, and is therefore inseparable from guilt, which arises inevitably from the operations of the will. Driven by this determinist pessimism, bourgeois tragedy reconciles us with our fate and advises submission to necessity by presenting powerless men and women crushed between rights of society and reasons of state.

Richard Wagner (1849)

[The Greek] hearkened to the great story of Necessity told by the tragic poet through the mouths of his gods and heroes on the stage. For in the tragedy he found himself again, – nay, found the noblest part of his own nature united with the noblest characteristics of the whole nation; and from his inmost soul, as it there unfolded itself to him, proclaimed the Pythian oracle. At once both God and Priest, glorious godlike man, one with the Universal, the Universal summed up in him: it were better to be for half a day a Greek in presence of this tragic Art-work, than to all eternity an – un-Greek *God*!

Wagner 1966: 34-5

Since 1848 German principalities have been in a state of unrest as people demand constitutional government. During the early months of 1849, Richard Wagner (1813-83) does not hesitate to risk his life-appointment as Royal Saxon Kapellmeister of the court orchestra as well as his emerging reputation as a composer by speaking in public against money and property, or personally circulating inflammatory articles which advocate the overthrow of the aristocracy. By spring, Dresden, the capital of Saxony, becomes the centre of a widespread cooperation of local republican forces with leftist activists of Central and East European countries. During the popular uprising of 3-9 May, which demands from the King justice and reform, Wagner supports the insurrectionists, joining in the streets his friend Mikhail Bakunin (1814-76), one of their leaders.

In the essay 'Art and Revolution', written just a month after the defeat of the Dresden revolt and his escape to Paris, Wagner explains why art must be liberated from capitalist considerations so that it can blossom and disclose the aspirations of emancipated humanity. Presenting Art as a social product, he seeks its role in the life of the State. To that effect, he conducts a survey of the worldly place of art from antiquity to the present. His models are the Greeks, who developed a democratic State, procreated Art, gathered in the theatre to probe its tragic depth, and established the popular assembly as its judge. Speaking of the individuals attending such performances in the theatre he exclaims that 'it were better to be for half a day a Greek in the presence of this tragic Art-work, than to all eternity an – un-Greek *God*!' Drama, the perfect work of art, was the epitome of all that was expressible in Greek society. Athenian State and Tragedy developed together, and hand in hand marched to their downfall. 'As the spirit of *Community* split itself along a thousand lines of egoistic cleavage ...; and, at the bitter end, every impulse of Art stood still before Philosophy, who read with gloomy mien her homilies upon the fleeting stay of human strength and beauty. To *Philosophy* and not to Art, belong the two thousand years which, since the decadence of Grecian Tragedy, have passed till our own day' (34). Art may have served various abstract ideas and conventions but never more was she the free expression of a free community since there has been no such community.

> With the subsequent downfall of Tragedy, Art became less and less the expression of the public conscience. The Drama separated into its component parts; rhetoric, sculpture, painting, music, &c., forsook the ranks in which they had moved in unison before; each one to take its own way, and in lonely self-sufficiency to pursue its own development. And thus it was that at the Renaissance of Art we lit first upon these isolated Grecian arts, which had sprung from the wreck of Tragedy. The great unitarian Art-work of Greece could not at once reveal itself to our bewildered, wandering, piecemeal minds in all its fullness; for how could we have understood it.
>
> Wagner 1966: 52

In its contemporary quandary, modern art is the docile handmaid of Mercury, Roman god of commerce: its ethics is profit, its essence industry, its purpose the entertainment of a shallow audience. A comparison of the public art of modern Europe with that of Greece, which reached its zenith in Tragedy, shows that the latter 'was the expression of the deepest and the noblest principles of the people's consciousness: with us the deepest and noblest of man's consciousness is the direct opposite of this, namely the denunciation of our public art. ... The Greeks sought the instruments of their art in the products of the highest associate culture: we seek ours in the deepest social barbarism' (47). Beauty and Strength were attributes of public life and sources of Art, whereas today all people are slaves. Modern art needs to rebel so that its perfect artwork, Tragedy, will be born anew. 'But only Revolution, not slavish Restoration, can give us back that highest Art-work. ... If the Grecian Art-work embraced the spirit of a fair and noble nation, the Art-work of the Future must embrace the spirit of a free mankind, delivered from every shackle of hampering nationality' (53-4). It is for Art, and Art above all else, to teach this social impulse its noblest meaning, and guide it towards its true direction. And only on the shoulders of this great social movement can true Art lift itself from its present state of civilized barbarianism, and take its place of honour. Revolution and Art share a goal, and they can reach it only when they recognize it jointly. This goal is the strong handsome Man, to whom Revolution shall give his Strength, and Art his Beauty.

As for the stage as moral institution, 'so long as we look upon a theatrical institution as a mere means for the circulation of money and the production of interest upon capital, it is only logical that we should hand over its direction, i.e., its exploitation, to those who are well-skilled in such transactions; ... if the Theatre is at all to answer to its natural lofty mission, it must be completely freed from the necessity of industrial speculation' (61-2). Furthermore, its priority over all other artistic institutions in this emancipation must be acknowledged, given its wide reach, weighty influence and lofty mission. The enfranchisement of public art would be a first step. The State and the Community ought to adjust their means to this end so that the Theatre, freed from the fetters of commercial speculation, can obey only its higher and true calling. The judge of its performance will be 'the free public. Yet, to make this public fully free and independent when face to face with Art, one further step must be taken along this road: the public must have *unbought* admission to the theatrical representations' (63-4). The ultimate ideal to pursue is one of perfect union: as people unite under the inevitable conditions of the approaching revolution, art and education will merge and they will become artists. And as they join together in free service for Art, its institutions will announce the standard for all future communal institutions. The noble human faculties will give humanity's social bearing its true artistic nature. In effect, the composer's socialist convictions reintroduce to the dramaturgical problematic the ethico-political questions first raised by Schiller during his republican years.

Wagner returns explicitly to the project of his Romantic predecessor in his book *Opera and Drama* (1852), where he shows that the dramatic creativeness of Schiller is swaying between the perfect form of Greek drama and History and Romance, trying to afford a halfway-house between ancient and modern understanding. Germany has had a Luther but not a Shakespeare. Schiller began by working on domestic and political Romance but later aspired to turn drama to naked History, and in the end tried myth as well but could not decide between the two. His impasse still defines the options of German theatre.

> Thus Schiller stayed hovering between heaven and earth; and in this hovering hangs, after him, our whole dramatic poetry. That heaven, however, is really nothing but *the antique art-Form*, and that earth, *the practical Romance of modern times*. The newest school of dramatic poetry – which, as *art*, lives only on the attempts of Goethe and Schiller, now turned to literary monuments – has developed the aforesaid hovering between opposite tendencies into a positive reeling.
>
> Wagner 1995: 147-8

So long as this is unresolved, '*we have no Drama, and can have no Drama*' (150-1). Historical Romance develops mechanically inwards from without while Drama grows organically outwards from within. Historical Drama forged by modern Romance shows that History is unsuitable for Drama. Today, Romance has turned into Journalism, and poetry has become political appeals to the people. These developments reflect the modern predicament: politics is our fate, poeticizing is politicizing. The Poet will not be able to work on Drama again till there is no more Politics. His present task is to present the struggle through which individuals attempt to free themselves from religious Dogma and the political State. In addition to Drama proper, these times lack the real enabler of the performance, the Public, since the advancing degradation of the audience has passed the rule of taste to the Philistines. But the artist of the present can see and announce the unborn life of the future. That life will emerge from the self-realization of Society's belief in its purely human essence, and will have no Dogma and only one universal Religion, the common conscience vindicating true human nature. Greek fate was the inner Nature-necessity while the modern one is the outer necessity of the arbitrary political State. This State lives on the vices of society, trying to equalize its imperfections. But the imposition of such a general norm works against human individuality from which virtues are solely derived. Society should instead be organized on the basis of such free individuality whose essence is natural necessity so that the self-determining individual will become its source. The State, which has denied humans such freedom, should be annulled.

Karl Marx (1852)

Hegel remarks somewhere that all great world-historical facts and personages occur, as it were, twice. He has forgotten to add: the first time as tragedy, the second time as farce. Caussidière for Danton, Louis Blanc for Robespierre, the Mountain of 1848 to 1851 for the Montagne of 1793 to 1795, the Nephew for the Uncle. And the same caricature occurs in the circumstances in which the second edition of the Eighteenth Brumaire is taking place.

Men make their own history, but they do not make it just as they please; they do not make it under circumstances chosen by themselves, but under circumstances directly found, given and transmitted from the past. The tradition of all the dead generations weighs like a nightmare on the brain of the living. And just when they seem engaged in revolutionizing themselves and things, in creating something entirely new, precisely in such epochs of revolutionary crisis they anxiously conjure up the spirits of the past to their service and borrow from them names, battle slogans, and costumes in order to present the new scene of world history in this time-honored disguise and this borrowed language. Thus Luther donned the mask of the Apostle Paul, the Revolution of 1789 to 1814 draped itself alternately as the Roman Republic and the Roman Empire, and the Revolution of 1848 knew nothing better to do than to parody, in turn, 1789, and the revolutionary tradition of 1793 to 1795.

> Marx, *The Eighteenth Brumaire of Louis Bonaparte*,
> quoted in Tucker 1978: 594-6

Marx's life-long classical learning has been thoroughly documented (Prawer 1976). The opening pages of *The Eighteenth Brumaire of Louis Bonaparte* (1852) draw on this learning to capture the theatricality of history. Even though the epigraph above does not articulate an explicit view of the tragic, it is quoted here for its masterful rhetoric and its stark portrayal of human destiny. It would not be easy to claim that these pages have been superseded philosophically or stylistically.

Friedrich Nietzsche (1872)

Of this foundation of all existence – the Dionysian basic ground
of the world – not one whit more may enter the consciousness
of the human individual than can be overcome again by this
Apollinian power of transfiguration. Thus these two art drives
must unfold their powers in a strict proportion, according to the
law of eternal justice.

Nietzsche 1967: 143

Friedrich Nietzsche (1844-1900) meets Wagner and is converted to
his theories in 1868. The two men will stay in close, exhilarating
contact for eight years till after the first Bayreuth Festival when they
will have their last meeting and tacit rupture. The philosopher's first
major book, *The Birth of Tragedy out of the Spirit of Music* (1872), is
deeply motivated by Schillerian aesthetics as absorbed by Wagner
who, Nietzsche thinks, is related to Schopenhauer as the poet to
Kant. It returns to Schiller's two major questions and 'starts out
from essentially the same problems that occupied the poets of
German Classicism, the problem of tragedy as a joyful vision of
suffering and the problem of drama in general as a communal art
form' (Bennett 1979: 245). The book explores the conditions under
which tragedy arose, evolved, declined and died, and the possibility of
its modern rebirth. Regarding the latter, Nietzsche joins the long line
of those who for a century have been arguing that, if the English
have Shakespeare and the French court drama, the Germans need
their own national theatre. Wagner has shown the possibility of such
a theatre. As for origins, how was it possible, he asks, for the Greeks
to endure the cruelty of nature and history, deriving delight rather
than resignation? How is it that contemplating pain and suffering in
tragedy still provokes a positive response in the audience?

While some see this effect as 'moral delight', Nietzsche dismisses
the attempt to incorporate moral claims into art. Art must be pure,
must contain its own explanation. Dispensing with fear and pity, and

rejecting Aristotelian catharsis, he treats pleasure peculiar to tragic suffering as aesthetic pleasure whose source lies in the aesthetic sphere, the *Schauspiel*/spectacle of an artistic *Spiel*/game that the will plays with itself. Only the metaphysics of art can explain why 'existence and the world seem justified only as an aesthetic phenomenon' (Nietzsche 1967: 141). He rejects everything traditionally associated with pain and loss, anguish and pessimism, and finds drama poised between an awareness of chaos and a will to form, between process and structure. 'This *movement* from chaos to form *and back* distinguishes Tragedy from other forms of *poiesis* (such as the epic and lyric) and from all *systems* of knowledge and belief (such as science and religion). All other prospects on human existence tend to freeze life in an apprehension of either chaos or form; only Tragedy requires a constant alternation of the *awareness of chaos* with the *will to form* in the interest of life' (White 1973: 340). The effect of tragedy out of this tension is 'an overwhelming feeling of unity leading back to the very heart of nature. The metaphysical comfort – with which, I am suggesting even now, every true tragedy leaves us – that life is at the bottom of things, despite all the changes of appearances, indestructibly powerful and pleasurable' (Nietzsche 1967: 59) is what made it possible for the Greeks to look boldly into terrible destructiveness and comfort themselves. On the last page of his book, Nietzsche has Aeschylus respond to Schelling's question about the Greeks bearing the contradictions of tragedy: 'how much did this people have to suffer to be able to become so beautiful!' (144). Nietzsche appreciates tragedy as the greatest aesthetic phenomenon, praising its beauty and stressing it joy of life. 'Art is "*the* metaphysical activity" of "life"; it defines the way in which beings as a whole are, insofar as they are. The supreme art is the tragic; hence the tragic is proper to the metaphysical essence of beings' (Heidegger 1981: 26). Nietzsche turns aesthetics into metaphysics.

What is the tragic? It is a complex ethical category that pertains to demands for justification (Pippin 1997: 316) following the recognition of suffering and the temporality of human existence. Force and justice (to use Lucien Goldmann's terms) are already in conflict in Winckelmann's description of the Laocoon, a statue (also discussed in Schiller's essay 'On the Pathetic') which after all depicts punishment and raises the question of justice. If there is no moral justification for pain and no religious comfort for anxiety, can life still make sense?

> 'Has existence a meaning?' is, according to Nietzsche, the highest question of philosophy, the most empirical and even the most 'experimental' because it poses at one and the same time the problems of interpretation and evaluation. Strictly speaking it means 'what is justice?' and Nietzsche can say without exaggeration that the whole of his work is an effort to understand this properly.
>
> Deleuze 1983: 18

The oldest response to this shattering recognition came during the tragic era of the Greeks, who perceived the paradoxical nature of identity and confronted it by exposing its fragility on the stage.

Nietzsche's approach belongs to the doubling of Greece, which has a long German tradition (Lambropoulos 1993: 174-7). This tradition believes that there have been two Greeces, one of light and law, beauty and balance, and an opposite one of mystery and mysticism, death and darkness. The two are often represented by Apollo and Dionysus, the gods who are set up as supreme types of ideal beauty in Winckelmann's *History of Ancient Art*; as symbols of restraining and unrestrained power in Schelling's *Philosophy of Revelation* (1858); and as the forces of clarity and repose vs materiality and exuberance (Arnott 1984: 139-40) in *Mother Right* (1861) by Nietzsche's friend Johann Jakob Bachofen. Wagner mentioned the two gods in the opening of 'Art and Revolution' (1849) and discussed them with Nietzsche and his friend Erwin Rohde in 1870. The young classicist embraced the double view early on. 'And in general, wherever one looks in Nietzsche's historical pageants, those Greeks who are supposed to be most representative of privileged moments turn out to be not teeming with historical possibilities but ambivalent, Janus-faced, and transitional figures, filled, whether they recognize it or not, with a foreboding of their own imminent or actual decline' (Porter 2000: 229).

In Nietzsche's cosmological view of the double Greece, the oppositions expressed by the two divinities now include Olympian–chthonic realm, light–darkness, measure–excess, security–freedom, sculpture–music, individualism–loss of self, order–violence, calm–ecstatic attitude, repose–intoxication, dream-like–mystical disposition. Here is how he contrasts the two in a notebook of 1885-6: 'Fundamental psychological experiences: the name "Apollonian" designates the enraptured lingering before a fabricated, dreamed-up world, before the world of *beautiful illusion* as a redemption from *becoming*. Dionysos, on the other hand, stands namesake for a becoming which is actively grasped, subjectively experienced, as a raging voluptuousness of the creative man who also knows the wrath of the destroyer' (Nietzsche 2003: 80-1). While the former desires an eternity of appearances in order to fabricate being, the latter pushes towards the creation and annihilation of becoming. The two are inextricably linked.

As the god of appearances, Apollo corresponds to Schopenhauer's representation while Dionysus symbolizes the notion of the will. But while for Schopenhauer tragedy led to renunciation, for Nietzsche it does not make the Greeks abandon the will to live. 'It saved them by teaching them to affirm without reservation what could have led them to renunciation, pessimism, or nihilism. *The Greeks had art in order not to deny life as a result of the disclosure of the contradiction of the will*. Their Dionysian music, their tragedies, affirmed life in spite of its contradiction' (Taminiaux 1993: 123). The contradiction between Apollo's demand for boundaries and Dionysus's drive for excess was transcended through dramatic unity. That is why Nietzsche speaks passionately about his predecessor's aesthetics of music but not at all about his theory of tragedy. Following the revelation of a purposeless universe, tragedy does not serve the negation of the will but has the opposite effect of justifying existence.

In short, the achievement of Greek tragedy, according to Nietzsche, was, first of all, to confront its spectator directly with the fact that there is just one world, the world we live in, the chancy, arbitrary but also rich and beautiful world of nature. It is not redeemed by any 'beyond'; nor is it given even the sort of *negative* meaning, in relation to a beyond, that it is given in Christian tragedy. Nietzsche throughout his life finds it amazing that the Greeks should have been able to confront so truthfully the nature of life, without flight into religion of the world-denigrating resignationist sort. He finds an explanation for this unique courage of affirmation in the structure of the tragic art.

Nussbaum 1991: 102

Apollo helps develop the sufferings of Dionysus into drama, brings dark forces into life, invests the tragic with beautiful appearances, and gives aesthetic meaning to metaphysics. Harmony results from the conflict of opposing forces. Tragedy presents not their reconciliation but their precarious balance as the two opposing forces struggle to resist or assimilate the other. 'A main reason for Nietzsche's continuing admiration of the Greeks is what he takes as their ability to exploit mechanisms of this sort. Having glimpsed the truth, ... they were, according to his unsettling view, revolted by it. Accordingly, they turned away from its pursuit. They made the preliminary stages of its conquest their final purpose' (Nehamas 1985: 119).

Nietzsche hopes that a rejuvenated combination of philosophy and tragedy will usher in a new tragic era, with the former taking the lead this time: 'Philosophy has to produce the need for tragedy' (Nietzsche 1979: 153). In 1850 Wagner believed that *The Ring* would usher in the revolution; twenty years later, in the same utopian vein, Nietzsche is convinced that philosophy will do the same for tragedy. He advocates a heroic philosophy that will be superior to the Greek because it will be consciously and explicitly tragic. For this to happen, the notion of the tragic needs to be liberated from theories of guilt, bad conscience, remorse, resentment and asceticism. The tragic does not live in fear or punishment; neither does it lament the injustice of suffering. Among Heraclitean concepts, it stresses play more than hubris. It accepts the saying which expresses the combination of the Apollinian and the Dionysian in *Prometheus Bound*: 'All that exists is just and unjust and equally justified in both' (1967: 72). Tragic wisdom acknowledges that on the stage of *Weltspiel*/worldplay cosmic justice consists in that higher justification of all that exists in its proportionately conflictual nature.

Maurice Maeterlinck (1896)

Is it beyond the mark to say that the true tragic element,
normal, deep-rooted, and universal, that the true tragic element
of life only begins at the moment when so-called adventures,
sorrows, and dangers have disappeared?

Maeterlinck, 'The Tragic in Daily Life', quoted in
Gerould 2000: 383

The Symbolist dramatist Maurice Maeterlinck (1862-1949) changes
his theatrical views often but supports them always with elaborate
theoretical accounts. Early in his career, he writes his best-known
statement on theatre. He is reacting to the Naturalism promoted
through both drama and theory in the 1880s by older playwrights
like Émile Zola (1840-1902) and August Strindberg (1849-1912). In
the essay 'The Tragic in Daily Life' (1896), he identifies the tragic
element not in the extraordinary occurrence but in ordinary existence. Seeking the most authentic life, he valorizes the self-contained
soul over restless immensity, destiny over adventure, fatality over
danger, murmur over tumult, mystery over violence. Maeterlinck
marvels at the obscure act of living and follows the uncertain,
dolorous footsteps of being as it attempts to reach the essence of intimate infinity through truth, beauty or God.

In this inert universe, nothing 'important' happens. There is no
antagonism of forces. Neither the struggle of the same (desire vs
desire) nor the conflict of opposites (duty vs passion, reason vs senti-
ment) expresses its intensity. For the first time in the history of the
tragic, Maeterlinck rejects collision altogether. The character of his
tragic is neither material (as in Naturalism) nor psychological (as in
most of Symbolism) but ontological: it pertains to the daily tragedy of
plain being. Thus the author is awed by the terrible tranquillity of
stars and silence, the unsettling quiet of happiness, the rush of repose,
the grandeur of humble existence. His world view endows the
commonplace with solemnity, timidity with dignity, doubt with clarity.

Correspondingly, theatre should reveal all that is substantial in the mere presence of life. Maeterlinck complains that contemporary tragic theatre is anachronistic because it presents a primitive, brutal world of barbarian bloodshed. The sublimity of this tradition is loud, verbose and superficial. It does not communicate anything about the depth of experience. Does Othello's jealousy represent his truest life more than its motionless moments? After all, most Aeschylean tragedies are examples of static theatre without events or even movement, physical or even psychological. It is only under such twilight conditions that life itself can be depicted – the meditative individual face to face with the universe. The greatness of these tragedies inheres not in actions but in words, and not even words of the necessary dialogue but of the superfluous one that permeates silence. This suggestive dialogue of the 'second degree' is authentically addressed to the soul because it is graced with a mysterious beauty revealing the soul's unceasing striving towards its own truth.

Like others before him, Maeterlinck discovers a tragic depth in life. But his life is not extreme, heightened, challenged or destroyed. It just is. What makes this life tragic is its being life: a reflective state more than an agonistic character, a mode of existence more than a condition of suffering. Here nobody dies, nobody complains, nobody escapes.

With Symbolism, the second major rift in the history of modern Western theatre occurs. If at the end of the eighteenth century tragedy and tragic theory parted ways (that is, the two began to address different issues), at the end of the nineteenth century the theatrical and the dramatic begin to take separate paths too. Drama does not unfold on the stage or in action but in altogether different realms – the mind, the psyche, words, dreams, acts, pantomime. The search for counter-theatre produces a new dimension of the tragic, privileging the primordial sense over the metaphysical and existential ones.

Sigmund Freud (1900)

[Oedipus's] destiny moves us only because it might have been ours – because the oracle laid the same curse upon us before our birth as upon him. It is the fate of all of us, perhaps, to direct our first sexual impulse towards our mother and our first hatred and our first murderous wish against our father. Our dreams convince us that it is so.

Freud 1953: 262

To some, modern messianic thought (be it communist, psychoanalytical or deconstructionist), because of its totalizing scope, has no room for tragic experience, whereas to others it is precisely through the tragic experience that such thought encounters its contradictions (e.g. Hyman 1956, Lacoue-Labarthe 1993: 112-13). Whether his perspective is behaviourist or materialist, determinist or positivist, Sigmund Freud (1856-1939) belongs to the latter persuasion since, in sharp contrast to Maeterlinck, he sees collision everywhere as he elaborates through a steadfastly dualist approach a Hobbesian view of the theatre of life. Detecting primary aggressiveness, self-destructive tendencies and deadly clashes, he unveils the irrational foundations of the psyche.

During his self-analysis in 1897, the neurologist Freud, who had been in clinical practice since 1886 but was in the process of abandoning his therapeutic procedures, records a new observation: while we react to presuppositions of destiny as arbitrary when we watch modern tragedies, we are riveted by *Oedipus Rex* because each one of us, in germ and in fantasy, was once such a person, and our dream-fulfilment is transplanted into the horror of tragedy (Freud 1966: 265). In his book *The Interpretation of Dreams* (1900), Freud returns to the question of the 'tragic effect' and tries to explain the universal appeal of the same play. When we are moved by Oedipus, our response is not dependent upon the clash between freedom and destiny or human and divine will; we are moved because we too have been cursed before our birth to direct our first sexual impulse towards our mother and our first murderous wish against our father. We identify with his fate because we carry his curse. As his guilt comes to light, we become aware of our repressed sexual impulses, and ultimately our inner selves. His fall makes us realize that we live in ignorance of the drives that offend morality even though nature has forced them upon us. This interpretation of the play transfers Aristotelian anagnorisis from the stage to the auditorium, that is, to the audience's response of (self-)recognition. The tragic effect of the drama is to make us face the fact that we are born criminals, and are therefore constitutively guilty. Inescapable guilt (first introduced by Schelling in his examination of responses to Oedipus and embraced by Hölderlin and others) returns here again, this time with no revolt against destiny, no demand for justice, no challenge to necessity. This guilty will is not defiant because the Kantian quest for autonomy has been completely abandoned. In a thoroughly heteronomous world, where choice is impossible, self-governance would be a foolish idea. Under such conditions, even Schopenhauer's withdrawal is not an option: life consists in serving one's sentence for the originary crime.

Years later Freud adds that this 'amoral' ancient play 'has a certain resemblance to the progress of a psychoanalysis' (1963: 330). Operating like it, analysis has a comparable tragic effect as it reveals our guilt (not just unsaid or hidden but suppressed and even unsayable) and shatters us with horror. Indeed Freudian interpretation draws on the model of tragedy even though its narrative takes the form of a novel. The structuring of the psychic 'machine' through the positing of Ego, Id and Superego is constituted on the basis of Greek and Shakespearean drama. Principles play the role of gods, forming a configuration of roles which respond to one another by their opposition, setting forth the stages through which the hero (the 'I') 'will pass in order to find himself at the end in the inverse of his original position' (de Certeau 1986: 22). Thus psychoanalysis (which its founder considered alternatively as methodology and 'mythology') is the first tragic theory that aspires to work like tragedy and with similar effects, yet another sign of its literary inclinations.

It took Freud till the early 1920s to shed the persona of the physician working in physiology and to start writing as a seer engaged in social criticism. However, he had already exhibited a scepticism about the possibility of a just society, which was typical of conservatives at the turn of the twentieth century. In his anthropological fantasy *Totem and Taboo* (1913), he argues that 'the origins of religion, morals, society and art converge in the Oedipus complex' (Freud 1955: 156), that is, in mankind's sense of guilt acquired at the beginning of history over the double criminal intention (incest and parricide), the repression of evil impulses into the unconscious, and the struggle with responsibility.

But why had the Hero of tragedy to suffer? and what was the meaning of his 'tragic guilt'? I will cut the discussion short and give a quick reply. He had to suffer because he was the primal father, the Hero of the great primaeval tragedy which was being re-enacted with a tendentious twist; and the tragic guilt was the guilt which he had to take on himself in order to relieve the Chorus from theirs. ... In the remote reality it had actually been the members of the Chorus who caused the hero's suffering; now, however, they exhausted themselves with sympathy and regret and it was the hero himself who was responsible for his own suffering. The crime which was thrown on his shoulders, presumptuousness and rebelliousness against a great authority, was precisely the crime for which the members of the Chorus, the company of brothers, were responsible. Thus the Tragic hero became, though it might be against his will, the redeemer of the Chorus.

Freud 1955: 156

The Oedipal subject is a split one, torn between the structured conscious and the unruly unconscious as its drives are in contradiction with one another and its faculties in constant strife. By the time of *Civilization and Its Discontents* (1929), Freud can determine the general plight of humanity, pulled apart by 'the terrible necessity of the inner connection between civilization and barbarism, progress and suffering, freedom and unhappiness' (Marcuse 1955: 17): culture cannot control the instincts which rule civilization, and therefore remains always vulnerable to violence, caught in a tragic conflict with barbaric forces it tries to transcend. 'Freud constructed a view of *human civilization* as a tragic drama, as having originated in a tragic crime, the murder of the primal father by the primal band of sons. Civilization is a continuing tragic story, requiring for its success the control, renunciation, and repression of instinctual forces, especially aggression and sexuality, and thereby generating increasing amounts of guilt' (Simon 1988: 254). Therefore civilization itself requires therapy since the whole of mankind may have well become 'neurotic'.

Like many troubled minds of his generation driven to despair by the loss of ancestral faith and the disenchantment of learned reason, Freud strikes back by turning his 'cultural frustration' against the entire Western project: he discovers the tragic essence of life to reside in the fact that culture may refine humanity but cannot save it.

Fyodor Sologub (1908)

Tragedy tears away the world's enchanting mask, and where it seemed to us there was harmony, predetermined or created, it opens up before us the world's eternal contradiction, the eternal identification of good and evil and other polar opposites. It affirms every contradiction and to every one of life's pretensions, correct or not, it equally and ironically says *Yes!* To neither good nor evil will it say the lyrical *No!* Tragedy is always irony; it is never lyrical. We must stage it that way.

Sologub 1986: 115

Poet, novelist, dramatist and essayist Fyodor Sologub (1863-1927) combines ardent Schopenhauerian pessimism with a radical theatrical aesthetic in the piece 'The Theater of One Will' which he contributed to a collection of Russian Symbolist essays, *A Book about the New Theater* (1908). Sologub explains that child's play is our first theatre: it is partly everyday, partly symbolic. We know it is all pretending but we love the amusing rites of the game. More than its content, we enjoyed the ecstasy of oblivion and the intoxication of a new world. When we go to the theatre as adults, we seek the same experience: a rite whose fiery ecstasy takes us from a boring life to a transformative action. Ignoring this expectation, contemporary theatre wants to be a spectacle staged by professionals and performed by illusionists. But soon we the viewers will demand that we participate again in a mystery the way we used to be players in a children's game. We will seek to recover our lost innocence in a re-enchanted world. To help theatre answer to its higher calling, today 'the task of the theater worker – author of drama, director, actor – consists of bringing it nearer to ecumenical activity, to mystery play and liturgy' (Sologub 1986: 109) and moving it away from diverting amusement.

The path to liturgy leads through an accidental multitude to the totality of Me. 'Every unity of people has significance in so far as it leads to Me – from the vain-seductive disunity to genuine unity. ...

91

And thus there is only one who wills and acts in tragedy, which adds to the unities of action, place, and time the unity of the will's aspiration in the drama' (110). Theatre must overcome the disunited action of a will splintered among many places, conditions and mores. Maeterlinck's 'daily life' has no place on the stage. Behind the numerous masks of spectacle there is one eternal mystery being played out, one eternal liturgy being performed, one eternal dialogue being carried out. 'There are no different people, there is only one person, only one *I* in the whole universe, willing, acting, suffering, burning in an unquenchable fire, and from the fury of a horrible and ugly life saved in the good and joyful embrace of the universal comforter – Death' (111). Correspondingly, the stage should be ruled by only one, the will of the poet, the maker of this alternative world. 'Drama – like the universe, also the work of one design – is a work of one creative thought. Only the author presents the fate of the tragedy, the accident of comedy. Isn't his powerful will in everything? As he wishes, so it will be' (111). Vainglorious actors will be banished from the stage and so will be acting itself other than the even transmission to an enchanted viewer of the intentions of the maker who proclaims: 'I have raised worlds with a merry game – and I am victim and I am priest' (119). Together with the commercial actors, the contented bourgeoisie will be expelled from the theatre. The worthy audience for the drama of the author's will and the single actor performing it is one viewer resembling the prompter in his dark box. Scenery, lighting and the other elements of the stage ought to give form to 'the tragic play of fate with its marionettes' (118) where earthly masks fall away as a single will reveals and affirms itself triumphantly.

However, it cannot all bury itself in silence and solitude. Not for the supreme will the twilight of reflective isolation. Theatre gravitates towards tragedy, and it should become tragic, while incorporating comedy into it. Its rippling laughter generates rhythm which calls for dance, a choral dance which invites whirling participation as it brings people gushing onto the stage and demolishing the footlights. 'And so the crowd that came to watch will be transformed into a group dancing in a ring that has come to participate in the tragic drama' (121). Naked dancers transcend the earthly tragicomedy as their beautiful flesh shines in the light of communal liberation. The mystery of one will leads to the collective self-abandon of tragic dance.

In Sologub's work we encounter again the crisis of mimesis that gives rise to anti-theatrical dramatism: theatre is accused of complicity in a false enchantment, that of conventional bourgeois life, and is challenged to seek an alternative enchantment, that of transcendent experience. This applies to both dramatic practice and life in general. Harmony is the mask that hides the world's contradictions. Theatre's responsibility is to expose and affirm these contradictions rather than reinforce false harmony with its own spectacle. Out of the liturgy of one will the communion of choral dance will break free from the walls of the stage, recover the origins of tragedy, and celebrate the true harmony of rhythm. Art and life will once again become one. As modernist theatre is consumed by this vision during at least the first half of the twentieth century, catharsis takes absolute priority over mimesis. The tragic idea gives theatre an anguished sense of split identity and propels it on a quest for its double – a quest for a 'total', 'pure', 'poor', 'legislative' or some other theatre that can authenticate it, free it from representation and save it from civilization.

Georg Simmel (1911)

The great enterprise of the spirit succeeds innumerable times in overcoming the object as such by making an object of itself, returning to itself enriched by its creation. But the spirit has to pay for this self-perfection with the tragic potential that a logic and dynamic are inevitably created by the unique laws of its own world which increasingly separates the contents of culture from its essential meaning and value.

Simmel 1968: 46

Georg Simmel (1858-1918) opens his essay 'On the Concept and the Tragedy of Culture' (1911) by positing Hegel's distinction between subjective and objective spirit as the fundamental dualism of soul and structure within the realm of the spirit. If the soul is the essence of the individual, structures like custom, morality, religion, law, science, technology and art are the individual's material expression. Once these structures are created, they acquire autonomy and stability – a 'fixed but timelessly valid' (27) existence. Although such an autonomous existence was part of the individual's aspirations in creating them, this achievement triggers a strange tension within the life of the soul, within subjective life, whose running stream, 'restless but finite in time' (27), keeps flowing and changing all the time. Once human works are made, they are endowed with an independence that separates them from the soul of their maker. They now create their own universe, that of culture. In turn, the soul confronts culture in different ways, experiencing attraction or repulsion, fusion with or estrangement from its contents. Thus a division is created between soul and its works, which generates 'innumerable tragedies' (27). The question, then, arises as to how this separation can be overcome. For Simmel, that is the question of culture, which is 'lodged in the middle of this dualism' (27).

The source of the problem is the dialectical necessity of form itself. Soul is more-than-soul – it is also its pulsating capacities in their constant 'drive towards form' (28), towards a higher articulation of individuality. The inner drive of its organic evolution towards greater perfection demands the integration of its history and the manifestation of its destiny, which can be achieved only through form. This implies that soul is also less-than-soul since the soul by itself, without the help of forms, cannot find fulfilment.

Culture ameliorates the soul's deficiency and serves self-perfection by giving a meaningful direction to the drive towards form and by leading the life process to ever more advanced stages of unified development. 'Culture is the way that leads from the closed unity through the unfolded multiplicity to the unfolded unity' (29). Through its operations, singularities spread out, potentialities mature into actualities, drives converge into a path. Thus culture represents the synthesis of subjective and objective spirit. In Simmel's view, culture is both path and destination: its objective forms are both 'stations' through which the soul needs to pass and the material of that special quality acquired by subjective life during such a wonderful passage – the unique quality of cultivation which establishes harmony between the free human activity and its products, between the subjective and the objective spirit of cultural values.

However, the necessity of cultivation introduces 'the paradox of culture' (30) – the fact that subjective life can reach inner perfection only through extrinsic means, that individual cultivation requires objective culture. To the extent that it obeys the dialectical logic of the spirit, effecting a synthesis of the subjective and the objective, culture is the agent of that distinct human growth known as cultivation. The real paradox is the heteronomous development of the autonomous subject, the fact that the autonomy of the soul is violated by the heteronomous drive towards autonomous structures. What puzzles Simmel is the scandal of form. How can the soul's perfection be an inner one if it requires the assimilation of alien forms? Why should an attempt to posit subjective autonomy result in an admission of the objective autonomy of spiritual culture?

Despite culture's beautiful promise for a harmonious synthesis of subject and object, the iconolatric ignominy of forms, the paradoxical independence of representation, emerges to discredit the hope of union. By its very nature, the spirit is condemned to an eternally unfulfilled motion that first drives it towards objects and then, without allowing it to penetrate them, drives it back to its own orbit. There is no way out of this self-contained, cyclical motion. The mutual attraction and revulsion between subject and object continue unresolved. Thus the notion of overcoming and the ideal of fusion are abandoned. The division between subjective and objective spirituality is described in terms of resentment and hostility as the domain of culture begins to turn into a nightmare.

Simmel finds two forces at work in the unfolding of cultivation: a constructive one, where individual growth assimilates objective spirit, and a destructive one, where individual growth obeys the logic of forms. Thus culture presents humans with its conflicting demands. These demands are not extrinsic but lie at the heart of life itself since life has a dual function: as a process, it marches forward, unfolding and maturing according to its inner nature; as a creation, it produces objects with a distinct cultural logic that follow their own course of growth. The independence and stability of their existence put the flow of life at risk when life pursues its highest development, cultivation, and seeks to use them as means. If the flow passes through their domain, they threaten to arrest it. Thus human development needs both to create and to escape the power of its creations in order to avoid being extinguished by them. The achievement of permanence undermines the possibility of movement. Instead of cultivating it, spiritual forms can lead inner life into paralysis. By taking on a life of their own, external values can stifle the human capacity to confer value by objectifying its spirit. 'Herein lies one fundamental form of our suffering from our past, our own dogma, and our own fantasies' (31). Within 'the basic tension between the process and content of consciousness', the discharge of creative process and the fixed shape of works and norms are fundamentally opposed. The structures of life as creation can freeze the rhythm of life as process. Rhythm and structure are simply antithetical. The dualism of life and form is insurmountable. Form, created as a vessel for the spirit, turns into its coffin.

It is not the opposition between subjective and objective spirit that disturbs Simmel so much as the heteronomy of the former. Why should the soul, the source of all values, need contours and configurations, figures and formations to express itself? Why should the 'completely closed reality which we call our subject' (38) need those outside products of the objective intellect 'which have grown into an ideal existence' (36)? Why should cultivation be meaningful only when endowed with objectification? Why should the spirit be embodied?

According to Simmel, culture unifies subject and object by incorporating objective phenomena in the development of subjects as a means towards personal growth, that is, without compromising the objectivity of such phenomena. In this way, the spirit reaches perfection in subject and object, enabling both of them to transcend their materiality and become respectively more-than-life and more-than-construct. Thus culture is by definition a synthesis since it interpenetrates subjective and objective spirit, bringing together personal development and objective value. 'A synthesis, however, is not the only and most immediate form of unity, since it always presupposes the divisibility of elements as an antecedent or as a correlative. Viewing synthesis as the most sublime of formal relationships between spirit and world could occur only during an age which is as analytical as the modern' (35). Having contemplated cultural reconciliation once more, Simmel proceeds to denounce it by recalling the division it presupposes. This time, he historicizes this ideal, arguing that only the Moderns consider synthesis the highest form of unity and attribute to culture the power to transcend the division of the spirit and fulfil the dialectic. This ideal is nothing but a chimera that enables them to impose artificial unity where there is only separation and friction. Instead of a path or a destination, it is a beautiful, seductive lie. Instead of a solution, culture is the problem. It is clear that the tragic idea played a decisive role in the establishment of culture as a distinct object of study and speculation during this period.

As an example of the ineluctability of 'the tragedy of duality' (Aron 1965: 140), Simmel cites its survival in cases of over-specialization, where people excel in a certain skill or branch of knowledge without becoming truly cultivated (Simmel 1968: 39). Such a cleavage in the structure of culture is not just historical but foundational, turning the paradox of culture into a tragedy. There is a constitutive friction between the inner drive of human personality and the inner logic of its creations. The source of this tragic friction is now located not in the heteronomous drive towards objectification but in another drive, one towards subjectification. Since the time humans developed an internal frissure by positing a self for themselves, an unbridgeable gap opened up between interiority and exteriority.

> From the moment that man began to say 'I' to himself, and became an object beyond and in comparison with himself, from the same moment in which the contents of the soul were formed together into a centre point – from that time and based on that central form the ideal had to grow according to which everything connected with the centre point formed a unit, self-contained and self-sufficient. But the contents with which the 'I' must organize itself into its own unified world do not belong to it alone. They are given to it from a spatially, temporarily idealized realm outside; they are simultaneously the contents of different social and metaphysical, conceptual and ethical worlds.
>
> Simmel 1968: 40

Simmel identifies an original sin in the drive towards subjectification, which destroyed the unity of a single, undifferentiated universe. By positing an autonomous subjectivity, by seeking to know themselves as such, humans expose themselves to the temptations of several outside worlds. Exterior worlds of religious, social, philosophical and other structures and values always seek to draw humans into them, dissolve their individuality and make them obey their dictates. Some individuals manage to find a balance among those dictates by ordering them around themselves. 'The process of culture, however, compresses the parties of this collision into extremely close contact by making the development of the subject conditional on the assimilation of objective material. Thus the metaphysical dualism of subject and object, which seemed to have been overcome by the formation of culture, reappears in the conflict between subjective and objective developments' (40). Hence culture, instead of overcoming the division, makes its presence more acutely felt. Cultivation represents a fall and at the same time the tragic awareness of the separation inherent in metaphysics.

From Schiller to Marx, artistic creation was the model of non-alienated work, presenting the organic autonomy of the disinterested artistic sphere as an alternative to the modes of capitalist economy. Simmel is unwilling to grant art such immunity. His view is deeply pessimistic. The fact that the modes of production have left behind the cultural super-structure is not just a 'contradiction' but a manifestation of the basic 'tragic paradox'. Alienation does not inhere in labour alone but also in the area that was supposed to enlighten or redeem labour – in culture itself and the widening gap between subjective and objective culture. The contradictions of modern culture represent an intense dramatization of the constitutive conflict between life process and generated forms. Thus, what was earlier perceived as a historically specific phenomenon is elevated into the realm of an eternal tragedy of culture.

Simmel's choice of tragedy as the prototype of existential alienation carries strong connotations. In a tragic situation, the destructive forces are immanent: the necessity of annihilation is the logical development of the very structure that has produced it. Just as the forces destroying the tragic heroes and heroines do not come from the outside but from within, their nature fulfilling their unique destiny (the fall of the auto-posited subjectivity), the destructive power of forms shares the same origin with the constructive one of creativity. What makes the human relationship to cultural objects tragic is that their human-made objectivity acquires an independent norm of development which tears them away from the subject, and the subject from itself (in a manner that repeats the scene of its original sin).

In a coda that prefigures the Frankfurt School critique of mass culture, Simmel laments the 'adornment and overloading of our lives with a thousand superfluous items, from which, however, we cannot liberate ourselves; the continuous "stimulation" of civilized man who in spite of all this is not stimulated to expressions of individual creativity' (46). He views these cultural ills as consequences of 'the emancipation of the objectified spirit' (46), of its independence which leads it farther and farther away from its goal of cultivation. Form is emancipated but the soul cannot liberate itself. This is the tragic situation of culture that, instead of achieving a synthesis, carries its self-destructive fate within it from the beginning. Culture as means undermines culture as a goal. Overcoming develops its own duality

and turns against itself. It is this dialectical elaboration and abnega-
tion that Horkheimer and Adorno popularized later with their
'tragic' (Rocco 1996) interdependence of myth and reason in the
Dialectic of Enlightenment. It is also the same elaboration that
inspired Lukács to posit, as the last Left Hegelian quest for reconciliation, the concept of 'totality'. In both cases, Simmel's epitaph for
culture has been interpreted as the birth certificate of counter-
cultural *Bildung*.

This is how engagement with *Kultur* becomes *Kulturkritik* – an
intellectual response to the crisis of the times not through political or
ethical philosophy but through cultural opposition. Such strong
emphasis on culture reflects a combination of social discontent, a
sense of intellectual poverty, the decay of artistic individualism and
the triumph of bourgeois mediocrity. When the intellectuals feel that
the middle class has betrayed the social contract of *Bildung* by abandoning its spiritual responsibilities for the pleasures of popular taste
and morality, they barricade themselves within *Lebensformen*/life-
forms like the *Bund* and the *Gruppe*, transforming the public sphere
from an alternative democracy into a militant aristocracy (Struve
1973) and declaring 'war against the West' (Kolnai 1938) – a civil war
they fight using the sheer negative force of culture. Since they see
progress as spiritual decline, and politics as moral failure, they are
determined to resist cultural disintegration, political anarchy and
social anomie by investing in art not for art's sake but as the only
meaningful way of life – as pleromatic experience. 'Forming a type
quite opposite to "civilization's literary man" driven by the itch to
reason and reform, the authentically German intellectual would
embody the "suprapolitical, powerfully ethical moment" of Kultur,
would be that paradoxical representative figure, the "unpolitical
man"' (Thomas Mann in 1918, quoted in Mulhern 2000: 6-7).

Driven by spiritual views of history, certain intellectuals replace
the demonic of the Romantics with chiliastic visions (Martin
Heidegger's adventism, Walter Benjamin's messianism, Georg
Lukács's totality, Ernst Bloch's 'not yet'), which prefigure religious,
aesthetic and national redemption. In the simultaneous critiques of
several grand systems (from parliamentarianism to Wagnerism, from
Neo-Kantianism to capitalism), synthesis is rejected as totalitarian,
being is presented as absolutist, while the unmitigated élan of

becoming surfaces as an open-ended goal. The new philosophy of heroic vitalism, revolutionary despair and conservative nostalgia does not offer the vision of a reconciled civilization in repose but calls to arms the defenders of an embattled *Kultur*. It is time for cultures to either decay or clash. This well-documented path from aesthetic discontent to political pessimism to nihilist activism leads to the first creation of cultural politics – an allegorical politics not of governance, morality, truth or beauty but of expressive, injured and defiant native authenticity.

Georg Lukács (1911)

> God must leave the stage, but must yet remain a spectator; that
> is the historical possibility of tragic epochs.
>
> Lukács 1974: 154

With his essay 'The Metaphysics of Tragedy' (1911), Georg Lukács
(1885-1971) responds to Simmel (with whom he studied in Berlin in
1909-10), expressing the modern demand for tragic form and insight
in uncompromisingly metaphysical terms: 'The question of the possibility of tragedy is the question of meaning and essence. It is the
question whether everything that is there, *is* – just because, simply
because, it is there. ... Is "being" a property of all things, or is it a
value-judgement upon things, a distinction and differentiation
between them?' (Lukács 1974: 156) And if indeed, as the author
clearly hopes, 'being' is a value-judgment upon things conferred
through distinction between them, what makes such a judgment
valid? A certain kind of theatre provides the answer. The paradox of
tragedy is that it creates real human beings by giving them sensual
form, and makes essence come alive. This miraculous creation of
reality takes place before the face of God. For Lukács, 'every true
tragedy is a mystery play. Its real, central meaning is a revelation of
God before the face of God' (154). The 'tragic miracle' is the coming
into being of a unique experience, an experience of new birth (and
already given tragic death), of autonomous, integrated selfhood.
'Tragedy is the becoming-real of the concrete, essential nature of
man' (162). It constitutes an exemplary case of being's differentiation.

In tragedy, 'the deepest longing of human existence' (162), the
longing for selfhood, can find its greatest satisfaction. The ecstasy of
mysticism cannot provide such satisfaction since at its peak, 'the
Unity of the All' (159), the mystic has to surrender his selfhood and
merge with all things into a melting flux of oblivion. Neither can the
necessity of history provide such satisfaction with its sense of arbitrary tyranny, just yet inexplicable fate, which presents life as a

102

regular accidentality. Mysticism deprives being of its uniqueness, its differentiation, while history denies it its value, its distinction. Only tragedy can respond to the question of meaning, the question of justification, the question of the ethical value of being. Only tragedy can pass an ethical judgment upon humans that properly differentiates their value.

But if neither ecstasy nor history can provide an appropriate set of criteria, where does tragedy find the principles to establish a 'hierarchy of life-possibilities' (173)? Within its own nature, answers Lukács, as a form-giving literary expression. 'Form is the highest judge of life. Form giving is a judging force, an ethic; there is a value-judgement in everything that has been given form' (173). In his contemporary essay 'Sociology of Modern Drama' (1911), Lukács argues that modern drama cannot solve its problems until a new ethical centre, like the one shared by the classical dramatist and his audience, is discovered. In this essay, with its very limited sociological concerns, he discovers such a centre not among social norms but in drama itself, where 'form has become the goal of life, a categorical imperative of greatness and self-perfection' (174). The new ethic is not located in society or religion, in communal beliefs or political practices. It is not even explored within an interpretive or performative framework where creator and audience can interact. It is simply identified with aesthetic entelechy, in this case, with tragic form. Tragedy finds its criteria within its own conformation, which is the ultimate judging force. A self-referential form 'which has been purified until it has become ethical' (174) has the authority to pass judgment upon meaning and the value of being.

Thus tragedy is not expected to work as a play or even an exemplary artwork. It is expected to do more, to perform a greater task, and this accounts for philosophy's great interest and belief in it. Tragedy is charged with the task of transcending text, performance, communication, art itself, and expressing a greater truth, a deeper insight into the depths of human existence – with solving the problem of essence. Consequently, the interpretive question of its meaning leads to the philosophical question of its possibility. There are other literary or art genres in general whose survival or continuity have been examined sociologically, culturally or aesthetically. Still, the survival of the ode, the opera or ornamentation has not been invested with as much significance as that of tragedy. As can be gleaned from Lukács' essay, only tragedy among all the kinds of art is expected to be more than a genre, more than an aesthetic category, more than an artistic accomplishment. Only tragedy is expected, in addition to becoming great art, to transcend its artisticality and perform a higher task: to become truly tragic. This task, which Lukács calls the 'metaphysics of tragedy', is ultimately an ethical one. 'Aesthetics are here – as in many other works of literary criticism by Lukács – intimately linked to an ethical standpoint, a moral position toward the life and the society of his time' (Löwy 1991-2: 126).

The possibility of tragedy is the possibility of an ethical art, an art that is more then mere art and assumes an ethical function. Tragedy cannot simply exist as any other genre. First, it has to appear in the world as an exemplary one. That is why, whereas mediocre novels or poems may be tolerated, average tragedies cannot. Tragedy must be either great or not at all. If it is not great, if it does not overwhelm its audience, it is reduced to drama. It may be excellent but still remains (bourgeois, naturalistic, symbolist or historical) drama. Second, tragedy must not just be great drama but must also make a qualitative leap outside drama and elevate itself to something higher than high art, truer than history, more mysterious than religion, more complex than politics. Tragedy must be greater than the genre of tragedy: it must be tragic.

Lukács is trying to restore to the theatre the moral authority which Schiller attributed to it and Nietzsche rejected with derision. He identifies the new ethical centre with the form of tragedy: tragedy finds its ethical criteria immanently, within its own form, the categorical imperative of greatness. This is also where he seeks the tragic: 'Dramatic tragedy is the form of the high points of existence, its ultimate goals and ultimate limits' (Lukács 1974: 159). Such high points occur suddenly, when the flow of empirical life is interrupted by 'the accident, the great moment, the miracle; an enrichment and a confusion' (153). These great moments of accidental insight are like epiphanies which impart illuminating knowledge. 'There, at the point to which the miracle of accident has raised a man and his life, tragedy begins. ... It begins at the moment when enigmatic forces have distilled the essence from a man, have forced him to become essential; and the progress of tragedy consists in his essential, true nature becoming more and more manifest' (155). The miraculous moment of the precipitate encounter with the accident brings into life a unique experience. This tragic experience, which occurs completely outside temporal existence, has an absolute unity of time in that it lasts only a fleeting moment; an absolute unity of force in that it happens suddenly and all at once; an absolute unity of meaning in that it makes everything essential; and an absolute unity of purpose in that its happening and its goal coincide, cancelling any expectation of development. What follows it is only manifestation. That is why Lukács concludes that 'the miracle is fulfillment. It snatches from life all its deceptive veils, woven of gleaming moments and infinitely varied moods. Drawn in hard and ruthless outline, the soul stands naked before the face of life' (153).

In addition to being a fulfilment, though, the great moment is also a failure because the wisdom imparted by the tragic miracle is the experiencing of the frontier between life and death which alerts the soul to its limits and brings it to self-consciousness. 'This is why tragedy is the awakening of the soul. The recognition of the frontier extracts the soul's essential nature' (161-2) and enables man to fulfil his longing for selfhood. Thus within tragic form Lukács discovers the tragic, the miracle of accident which both fulfils the longing for selfhood and advises the soul of its boundaries, thus bringing it to consciousness and making the essential human nature concrete. At a time of godlessness like the present, when, contrary to Simmel's hopes, form-destroying mysticism is no longer available and history constitutes a 'value-denying necessity' (167), when lonely souls wander through deserted paths in soulless nature and blind fate, tragedy emerges as the only metaphysics that can endow life with meaning, that can give the solitary souls a form in a reality of its own creation. The ethical form of the mystery play (tragedy) is contrasted to the undifferentiated flux of oblivion (mysticism) and the arbitrary pattern of fate (history).

This is, then, the ethical task of tragedy: to give form, expression, actuality to the modern longing for selfhood left homeless, voiceless by mysticism and history, faith and fate. With God as a mere spectator, and chance as an arbitrary tyrant, form assumes the authority of a judging force, and through its very actualization offers value judgments, making meaning possible again. Form purged of all teleology and application until it has reached the purity of self-contained ethics becomes 'the goal of life' (174), transposing the deontology of Kant's First Critique ('a categorical imperative') to the realm of the Third ('self-perfection'). 'Modern discussions of the possibility of tragedy are not exercises in literary analysis; they are exercises in cultural diagnostics, more or less disguised' (Sontag 1966: 132). This possibility is not a question of mere literary or even artistic importance but a central concern regarding human essence and expression, according to Lukács. There is something fundamentally human that is enunciated in tragedy, and that human quality is the tragic. What makes tragedy great is an extra-aesthetic quality, a form whose judging force differentiates authentic being – its ethical weight. It appears that it is the only genre, indeed the only kind of artistic creation, with an immanent ethical substance which is usually called 'the tragic'. While moral issues and positions may find expression in all other genres, it is only in tragedy that ethical choices must necessarily be made and carried to their ultimate (tragic) consequences. This gives it its unique moral urgency and intellectual potency. Tragedy is the domain of the ethical will.

Therefore the possibility of tragedy, the prospect of great tragedy, requires the practices of the ethical will, the self-legislating exercise of moral freedom. But the autonomy of this will, the integrity of selfhood that would satisfy the longing for being, can become problematic if their immanence is not defined in terms that make a forceful struggle possible. However, from the very beginning of his essay, Lukács specifies that the domain of the ethical will is a stage where the drama of human fate is enacted with God as the single spectator. The divine, which classical tragedy had placed on the stage, has displaced the audience. Tragic struggle is no longer a heroic drama of gods and mortals presented before the citizen body but an epiphanic encounter with enigmatic forces occurring before (and confirming the presence of) God, where 'there is no difference between seeming and substance, appearance and the idea, event and destiny' (Lukács 1974: 153). What makes the accident a great moment, redeeming it from the flux of history and the arbitrariness of fate, is the overseeing eye of God. Although he is no longer part of the tragic proceedings, it is because God is watching that the miracle acquires its momentous power, making man essential and fulfilling his longing for selfhood. 'The god

of nature and destiny, who is always speechless and always unre-
deemed, brings forth the voice of the god who slumbers inside man,
the voice which, in life, has fallen silent; the immanent god awakens
the transcendental god into life' (154).

Commenting on this view in 1918, another student of Simmel's,
Ernst Bloch (1885-1997), who is also expecting another birth of
tragedy, concurs: 'In other words, God must exit the stage (for, we
would add, he does not exist, but may only be valid; there shall be
nothing but God), but a spectator he must still remain: as this is the
only kind of piety still possible, it is also the historical, the utopian
possibility for tragic ages, epochs without a heaven' (Bloch 2000:
219). In this view, the ethical immanence of tragedy is compromised
by a defining heteronomy, the watchful presence of god. The
antinomy of freedom and necessity is annulled. However, Lukács
does not pursue Bloch's resolution. By the time that the evolution of
theatre some twenty years later proves him right, and a new tragedy
arrives on the stage, ho has burned his plays and has discovered
through Marxism a more meaningful idea of history.

Vyachislav Ivanov (1912)

> The more persistently the age demands consciousness from art,
> the more certainly this art will gravitate toward theory.
>
> Ivanov 1981: 212

During the first twenty years of the twentieth century, the tragic idea, as reconfigured by Nietzsche, spreads rapidly to many languages, cultures and fields. Scholar, theorist and poet Vyacheslav Ivanov (1866-1949) attempts to integrate philology and literature into a Christian philosophy. He proposes a synthesis of Dionysus and Christ, based on aesthetic mysticism and supported by religious anarchism, which will reconcile individual self-affirmation with collectivity outside of social norms and institutions. 'For this reason, the most suitable forms for the synthetic drama would be a divine and heroic tragedy similar to that of the Ancients and a mystery more or less analogous to that of the Middle Ages' (1986: 120). He presents Dionysus as a precursor of Jesus, seeking to overcome Nietzsche by bridging culture and revelation, and attacks the philosopher's individualism by stressing the communal aspects of his dramatic theory.

In the essay 'The Essence of Tragedy' (1912), Ivanov distinguishes Apollo, the masculine principle of unity whose symbol is the monad, from Dionysus, the feminine principle of multiplicity whose symbol is the doublet or dyad. 'The god of structure, co-ordination and harmony, Apollo is the connective and re-uniting power; ... The god of disruption, Dionysos, by descending, sacrifices his divine integrality and wholeness ...' (1981: 211). The depiction of this opposition requires a dialectic art which reveals the dyad in the form of a monad, thus embodying thesis and antithesis, namely, Hegelian becoming. 'The concept of the dyad presupposes an initial, intrinsic unity, in which an internal opposition is revealed' (213). The warring forces are primordially fused in a single existence harbouring 'a certain duplicity within itself – not as an inner contradiction, but as an inner wholeness. Only as the energy concealed within it grows and is definitely revealed will it assume the masks of division and discord' (213). The action of this drama, the 'bifurcation of the original unity into internally warring energies' (214), is captured in the mysteries of Dionysus, who is split into the antinomic hypostases of victim (suffering god) and sacrificator (sacrificial god).

With his double nature and multiple images, Dionysus represents transformation, more specifically, creation as an act of suffering and sacrifice. His dyadic nature exemplifies the immanent dialectic of tragedy between identity and difference. In theatrical terms, the dialectic became manifest in the split of the circling dithyrambic chorus into the satyr play, which absorbed 'everything that had been disorganized, improvised, unruly and sportive' (216-17), and tragedy, which incorporated 'everything that was heroic, sepulchrally cere-monial and mournfully funereal, superb and portentous' (217). Tragedy does not exist when duality pursues reconciliation. 'On the contrary, it exists whenever something, capable of resolving the conflict, has occurred and exists, but two equal forces, contending, strive to repel and expel it, do not wish an outcome and harmony but blindly want self, nothing but self – to be themselves and in opposi-tion to one another' (219). It consists in agonistic doubling, internecine strife within a natural unity, 'the principle of dying continuously on behalf of a higher existence' (221).

Not only does the genre of tragedy teach this lesson; the history itself of the genre exemplifies it. The withdrawal of the tragic element from the Dionysian prototype cooled bacchanalian enthu-siasm but produced the art of tragedy as structure and proportion prevailed (220). The advancement of tragedy subdued the tragic but could not eliminate it since the tragic comes from life. As a living principle, it has survived often outside art only to find another form and return. As Ivanov argues elsewhere, the tragic has most recently appeared in a new genre, Dostoevsky's 'novel-tragedy', which closely resembles the prototype of tragedy since its author 'learnt the deepest secrets of human unity and human freedom: that life is basi-cally tragic, because man is not what he is' (1960: 5). Dostoevsky deals with the two components of human destiny, necessity and freedom, focusing on crime as the ultimate act of autonomous law and an infringement of the rules of society. Thus the tragic has been preserved to our time and will be handed down to future ages, going itself through tragic cycles of sacrifice and resurrection, art and life, or theory and art. In this course of events, consciousness of the genre represents death.

Miguel de Unamuno (1913)

The people does not want comedy but tragedy.
Unamuno 1954: 295

Truly human people do not want the consolations of comedy but the turmoil of tragedy, suggests Miguel de Unamuno (1864-1936), a Basque Professor of Greek at the University of Salamanca. This argument appears often in his novels, poems, religious essays and philosophical reflections. In *The Tragic Sense of Life in Men and in Peoples* (1913), he presents it in a discussion of Paul's dream of mankind's final solidarity, anacefaleosis (the fusion of all people in Christ) and apocatastasis (the return of all things to God), whereby everything is saved. In this vision, human consciousness, which is sickness (18), is overcome in God's divine consciousness (252) as Christians surrender themselves to Him. Here the author baulks: 'But in this final solidarization, in this true and supreme *Christination* of all creatures, what becomes of each individual consciousness? what becomes of Me, of this poor fragile I, this I that is the slave of time and space ... ?' (255). If the poor I (Lukács's self-hood) is absorbed and finds peace as time is redeemed and hope is fulfilled, Unamuno calls the prospect not the overcoming but the 'climax of the tragedy' (256): an eternity that deprives humanity of its future, a quietude that appeases longing, an arrival that cancels lack – all these represent sheer death. A life without tragedy would be meaningless, a presence outside time hopeless, a divine existence deprived of suffering empty. As Kierkegaard knew, Christianity requires the martyrdom of faith. 'An eternal purgatory, then, rather than a heaven of glory; an eternal ascent' (256). Tragedy is a condition from which mankind does not wish to be saved.

The path to eternal life passes through hopelessness, agony, disease. The world must be experienced at its fullest through passionate engagement with one's uniqueness. Truth is subjective, goals are self-posited and, as Heraclitus taught, reality is in perma-

111

nent flux. In this mysterious world of contingency, humans can affirm their existence by being true to themselves and can orient themselves towards the future by fighting dissatisfaction with determination, despair with perseverance, waiting with anticipation.

Unamuno identifies this attitude with a certain ethno-geo-religious identity and tradition: 'What I call the tragic sense of life in men and peoples is at any rate our tragic sense of life, that of Spaniards and the Spanish people, as it is reflected in my consciousness, which is a Spanish consciousness, made in Spain. And this tragic sense of life is essentially the Catholic sense of it, for Catholicism, and above all popular Catholicism, is tragic' (295). This native tradition has its own exemplary hero, 'a comically tragic figure, a figure in which is revealed all that is profoundly tragic in the human comedy, the figure of Our Lord Don Quixote, the Spanish Christ, who resumes and includes in himself the immortal soul of my people. Perhaps the passion and death of the Knight of the Sorrowful Countenance are the passion and death of the Spanish people, its death and resurrection. And there is a Quixotesque philosophy and even a Quixotesque metaphysic, there is a Quixotesque logic, and also a Quixotesque ethic and a Quixotesque religious sense – the religious sense of Spanish Catholicism' (296). The cult of Don Quixote is the proper national religion for the land of mysticism and Counter-Reformation, of concrete philosophy that crosses from religion into art, of Stoic metaphysics which cultivates Humanist philology.

The 'Conclusion' to this loose collection of essays is entitled 'Don Quixote in the Contemporary European Tragi-Comedy'. Unamuno insists that modern Europe is caught between two pairs of literary protagonists: Dr Faustus and Mephistopheles (introduced by Christopher Marlowe in 1604), and Don Quixote and Sancho Panza (introduced by Miguel de Cervantes in 1605). Faust, the product of the Renaissance and Reformation, is the 'tragic Doctor' who has studied all sciences only to conclude that he knows nothing. Renaissance and Reformation, the twin siblings, bring to humanity the great temptations of beautiful Helen – the upheavals of Revolution, the metaphysics of Europe and the inquisition of Culture. Those in the European periphery who, like the Spaniards, are scorned for their lack of philosophy and science respond with the sublime exemplar of the fool who achieves immortality by making

himself ridiculous. 'The greatest height of heroism to which an individual, like a people, can attain is to know how to face ridicule; better
still, to know how to make oneself ridiculous and not to shrink from
the ridicule' (315). It follows that philosophy should be the science of
the inward tragedy of life, a reflection upon the tragic sense of life,
like the tragedy of the soul of Don Quixote that expressed the conflict
between reason and faith.

The tragic sense of life embraces the impossibility of resolution
between intellect and heart, thought and feeling, logic and emotion,
knowledge and wisdom, book and soul, rationalism and foolishness,
scepticism and belief, doubt and ideal, despair and hope, negation
and affirmation, modernity and tradition, Renaissance and Middle
Ages, Reformation and Counter-Reformation, *Kultur* and
Catholicism, and the numerous other distinctions that appear everywhere in Unamuno. These polarities define the essence of life and
should not be reconciled. Their tension generates anxiety but also
leads humans to authentic existence. Much as he invokes them, the
author resists the temptations of immortality and refuses to take
sides: his polarities are not about rejecting evil.

The sceptic Pontius Pilate, the man of culture, cannot make a
mockery of the 'tragedy of Christ'. Logic, aesthetics and ethics
cannot reduce to *Kultur* the mockery that underlies the 'tragedy of
Don Quixote' (315-16). 'We are not concerned only with truth,
beauty, and goodness: we are concerned also and above all with the
salvation of the individual, with perpetuation, which those norms do
not secure for us' (319). The essence of Spanish Catholicism consists
in its being an economy of things eternal (320). Its medieval soul
preserves 'the spiritual inheritance which has come down from what
are called the Dark Ages. And Quixotism is simply the most
desperate phase of the struggle between the Middle Ages and the
Renaissance which was the offspring of the Middle Ages' (322). If
other peoples bequeathed books to *Kultur*, Quixotism left an alternative philosophy and religion – the ability to make one's soul the
battlefield of faith in affirmation and faith in negation. By choosing
'the life of inquietude and passionate desire' (322) for what is ratio-
nally absurd, Don Quixote rejects both faiths, reaches 'the most
tragic ridicule of all, the inward ridicule, the ridiculousness of a
man's self to himself' (323), becomes conscious of his 'tragic comic-

ness' (324), and triumphs over it without ever denouncing it. He overcomes the world by making himself ridiculous, laughing at himself, and enjoying the laughter.

The modern world needs the holy fool to fight objectification, alienation and reconciliation 'in order to bring in a new and impossible Middle Age, dualistic, contradictory, passionate' (326). Having contaminated himself with criticism, intellectualism and sentimentalism, Don Quixote must escape the fate of Nietzsche and Tolstoy by reaching through despair to the heroic fury of Giordano Bruno (328-9); he must cry aloud in the wilderness; he must re-awaken in people's souls the tragic sense of life. Opposites cannot be reconciled, anguish eliminated, or darkness dispelled. Honest individuals can only learn to navigate the fundamental conflicts of worldly life.

As much as Central European intellectuals who had lost their faith in civilization were investing their dim hopes in culture, their contemporaries from the European periphery, such as Spain and Russia, were disaffected with culture, a Protestant mechanism of control. Indeed they were declaring that, to them, the very terms of autonomy had been meaningless all along.

Max Scheler (1915)

In every genuine tragedy we see more than just the tragic event.
We see over and above it the permanent factors, associations, and
powers which are in the very makeup of the world. It is these
which make such a thing possible. In every tragic event we are
directly confronted with a definite condition of the world's
makeup without deliberation or any sort of 'interpretation'.

Scheler 1965: 7-8

During the 1910s, Max Scheler (1874-1928) works on a phenomenology of values, examining their structure as presented to moral
consciousness and criticizing Kant's formalist approach to ethics for
its emphasis on obligation. After publishing his treatise *Formalism
in Ethics and Non-Formal Ethics of Value* (1913), he complements
his exploration with individual ethical studies, such as one on the
tragic, which presents morality as the stage of struggle among
values.

Scheler is the first writer explicitly aware of the fact that by now
the tragic has a long philosophical tradition behind it. In this essay,
before establishing the nature of the phenomenon, he rejects a
number of approaches to the tragic. He will speak of no particular art
because the tragic cannot be limited to artworks. It is not an
aesthetic phenomenon but 'an essential element of the universe
itself' (3). Its effects on the audience need to be disregarded too:
psychological investigations cannot reach objective understanding
since experiences, such as pity and fear, vary historically. 'The tragic
is above all a property we observe in events, fortunes, characters, and
the like, and which actually exists in them' (3). As a feature of the
world's makeup, it remains perceptible to all ages regardless of the
emotions it may arouse. The tragic is next dissociated from interpretive understanding because it cannot result from a false
interpretation due to an uncivilized or bewildered response to the
world. It may be subject to many interpretations but is itself fixed

and undeniable. At the other end, there are illegitimate metaphysical accounts which take it for granted and from the start presuppose its resolution.

In contrast to all these approaches, Scheler places the tragic in his favourite realm of values and their relationships. It is not itself a value but 'appears in objects only through the interplay of their inherent values' (5). Eternal values in repose do not suffice; they need to enter history by interacting among themselves and being affected by circumstances and even destroyed by conflict. The emergence of the tragic requires acting and suffering, specifically, the annihilation of a positive value by a force which itself possesses this moral value. The tragic becomes manifest not in the catastrophe itself but in the course that the destructive value forces upon the other. 'The manifestation is, moreover, purest and clearest where objects of equally high value appear to undermine and ruin each other' (6). Effective tragedies depict the (Hegelian) clash of equally superior powers and duties, each one with its own intrinsic rights. A more intense tragic occurs when the struggle takes place within the same person, event or thing or even more so when it unfolds in one and the same power or ability, destroying a thing or quality as it brings it to the highest positive value. Perceiving such a combination of achievement and catastrophe leaves a devastating impression.

Though itself not a value, the tragic is both immutable and inevitable because it is rooted in the world's makeup and thus confronts us with conditions beyond any deliberation. Such conditions clear away all questions of responsibility, making a certain reconciliation possible: the objective character of the event induces contentment with existence and fills us with the repose of resignation. We come to terms with destruction and find peace by accepting that it is inevitable. There is no point in contemplating a better-made world.

When it comes to the entities engaged in moral struggle, Scheler is not very consistent as he talks about two values, or a value and an object, or two objects. Last, he proposes that the conflict happens not between values but between causal and value relationships. The course of the former disregards the latter as the operations of the world do not take into account the exigencies of values. 'The simple fact that the sun shines on the good and bad alike makes tragedy possible' (10). Tragedy would be unthinkable in a world operating on a system of laws oriented towards values, whether negatively or positively: a perfectly satanic or angelic world would cancel it. 'We see the tragic only when in one glance we embrace both the causality of things and the exigencies of their immanent values. ... The result is a clear insight into the independence of these two things. It is here that we may see the formal "background" of all tragedies' (10). The tragic comes into sight when we comprehend that, contrary to any ethical demands, values and laws are unconnected.

Recuperating the original terms of the Kantian autonomy project, we may also distinguish between causal and inner necessity. The latter marks the man of fate who follows its course, even after he has performed all the 'free' actions which might help him escape this predicament. 'Tragic necessity' is the inescapable, necessary catastrophe, one of transcendent causality that lies above freedom. Neither determinism of nature nor freedom of will can account for its intrinsic logic, its inner historicity which makes the destruction of value seem equally unpredictable and necessary. Thus the tragic does not allow for a clear attribution of guilt because the question itself cannot be personalized: in such a situation, heroines and heroes, driven by inner necessity, fulfil their duty nobly to the best of their abilities, and they appear blameless. 'Tragic guilt' is of a kind for which no one can be blamed and for which no conceivable 'judge' can be found (14). It emerges when justice necessitates the destruction of value, when guiltless and unavoidable annihilation appears just. 'The tragic misdeed is even definable as that which silences all possible moral and legal powers of judgment; and, on the other hand, every conflict is essentially untragic when by moral and legal lights it is seen to be obvious and simple' (14). In the latter case, moral guilt is based on the act of choice. Tragic guilt is not incurred – it happens to the tragic hero who follows his pure will and thus remains guiltless.

Oswald Spengler (1918)

The drama of the West is ordinarily designated *Character-Drama*. That of the Greeks, on the other hand, is best described as *Situation-Drama*, and in the antithesis we can perceive what it is that Western, and what it is that Classical, man, respectively, feel as the basic life-form that is imperiled by the onsets of tragedy and fate. If in lieu of 'direction' we say 'irreversibility', if we let ourselves sink into the terrible meaning of those words 'too late' wherewith we resign a fleeting bit of the present to the *eternal* past, we find the deep foundation of every tragic crisis. It is Time that is the tragic, and it is by the meaning that it intuitively attaches to Time that one Culture is differentiated from another; and consequently 'tragedy' of the grand order has only developed in the Culture which has most passionately affirmed, and in that which has most passionately denied, Time.

Spengler 1926: 130

As World War One is concluding with the defeat of Germany in 1918, Oswald Spengler (1880-1936), a high school teacher who has taken early retirement to concentrate on his writing, publishes the first volume of his massive *Decline of the West* (with the second following in 1922). The book proposes in sharply aphoristic style a new philosophy of history without hierarchy, centre or destination. Historical time is discontinuous, governed by inexplicable fate, not laws of causality. In this frame, cultures, which function like distinct organisms subject to inherent development, evolve organically towards fruition (namely, their unique civilization), decay, and die. The author develops a 'comparative morphology of cultures' as they grow into 'separate worlds of dynamic being' independently of each other and go in their unrepeatable way through the life cycle of a plant. Goethe's plant morphology provides a model for world history. Spengler identifies and compares to various degrees eight major cultures, insisting that time cannot provide any ultimate justification for human endeavour, which is condemned, even in its dazzling civilizational manifestations, to remain unconnected, and vanish.

At a time when the understanding of the tragic has reached a dead end in phenomenology and existentialism, Spengler gives it a new orientation away from ethics and towards history. The organic logic of the existence of cultures embodies their destiny. Each culture as a prime phenomenon possesses a special destiny-idea proper to itself and known by names such as the Greek Nemesis, the Arab Kismet or the Western Providence. The impact of destiny on a culture's basic life-form represents a shattering encounter with time and forces the recognition that the fleeting present becomes irreversibly eternal past. Spengler proposes that it is time itself that is the tragic, and therefore through such encounters each culture undergoes a unique crisis and develops its own tragic view. He illustrates this through extensive comparisons between the two cultures that have been most interested in this question, the time-denying, ahistorical Classical (Greco-Roman) one, which he calls (after Nietzsche) 'Apollinian', and the time-affirming, ultrahistorical Western one, which he calls 'Faustian' (a term Unamuno would fully approve) and dates since the Gothic Middle Ages. In the ancient world, which is steered by the illogical casual of the moment, Oedipus stumbles upon a situation, self-review is conducted as public action, and a story of Euclidean destiny is told by anecdotal drama. In the modern world, which is ruled by the inexorable logic of becoming, Lear matures towards a catastrophe, apology takes the form of an inward monologue, and a story of analytical destiny is told by biographical drama. The former, the tragedy of a mask, revolves around fate and occurrence, while the latter, the tragedy of a portrait, revolves around character and gesture. In the finite, immediate and local setting of Apollinian morning brightness, plastic columns of temples rise in static passivity; in the boundless, retreating, universal setting of Faustian evening twilight, musical spires of cathedrals rise in dynamic activity. The one establishes a material body, the other, an empty landscape.

Spengler's sharp polarities recall every differentiation between Ancients and Moderns, from Schiller's naïve and sentimental poetry to Lukács's archaic epic and bourgeois novel. Also, his style bears the traces of both his interest in Heraclitus (on whom he wrote a dissertation, receiving his doctorate in 1904) and his early dramatic fragments. Still, his innovation is to raise the issue of irreversible time itself, and of the inescapable decline which forces each culture to confront its inherent destiny, rather than freely determine its destination, and to play its role accordingly on the stage of world history. In the wake of his oracular dismissal of catharsis, time appears in need of redemption.

Franz Rosenzweig (1921)

> The silence of the tragic hero is silent in all art and is understood in all art without any words.
>
> Rosenzweig 1971: 81

When *The Star of Redemption* appears in 1921, Franz Rosenzweig (1886-1929) is head of the Free Jewish House of Study in Frankfurt. The book is a polemical attempt to settle once and for all the accounts of its author's generation with philosophy, Protestantism and Hellenism. It rejects all three in a move indebted to Schelling's teachings on history and revelation and to *Religion of Reason out of the Sources of Judaism* (1919) by Rosenzweig's teacher Hermann Cohen (1842-1918). Rosenzweig hopes to redeem time from Spenglerian contingency, from the uncontrollable flux which he discovered when he studied history and philosophy.

A significant component of the attack on Hellenism is the total rejection of the tragic idea. In his discussion of modern tragedy, Rosenzweig adopts Spengler's distinction between tragedy of action and of character (210): while in ancient drama action differed but heroes were always the same, in modern drama each hero has unique perspective. Also, the chorus (207), which used to represent the world addressing the hero, has become superfluous and disappeared because the modern hero, endowed with volition and mortality, is directly visible and audible, and needs no mediation. Dialogue, rather than monologue, predominates.

In an earlier section, though, 'Man and His Self or Metaethics' (book 3 of part I on the 'Proto-Cosmos'), Rosenzweig gives a lengthy description of the tragic hero, which is remarkable on two counts: first, it is inconsistent with the Spenglerian distinction (ancient action vs modern character) adopted elsewhere in the book, and second, it represents the very first assault on tragedy in the tradition of tragic thought spanning some one hundred and thirty years. Here Rosenzweig distinguishes between ancient self/character and

121

modern individual/personality. The former is driven by a metaethical (Heraclitean) *daimon*, the latter by an ethical soul. Action does not appear at all in this picture. In fact, Rosenzweig concentrates on antiquity, expanding selectively on Lukács's view of loneliness in drama (Lukács 1971: 45). Self-willed character is an inherently solitary man with no connections or relations, who spends his time in self-restriction and introverted confinement. Selves like him cannot converge and create a community because they are all mute, blind and deaf – rigid marble statues which demand immortality by remaining ever themselves. This is the speechless, sightless, motionless ethos of the pagan hero. As for his tragic predicament, 'the consciousness of antiquity did not account him culpable for rising up in defiant surges and staking out a character as such, but rather for holding fast to a particular character which was unevenly blended and which lacked harmony, so that some one element in it predominated and disturbed the good proportions. Only this congenital defect was the *hamartema* which necessitated the tragic fall of the hero' (Rosenzweig 1971: 212). This is Rosenzweig's portrait of the 'classical man', painted with passionate revulsion.

But the portrait does not function only as an indictment of the Greeks. It constitutes a total denunciation of art itself: 'The realm of art provides the ground on which the self can grow up everywhere; but each self is in turn a wholly solitary, individual self; art nowhere creates a real plurality of selves, although it produces the possibility for the awakening of selves everywhere: the self that awakes nevertheless only knows of itself. In the make-believe world of art, in other words, the self ever remains self, never becomes – soul' (81). Rosenzweig is uncompromising: he finds all art false and corrupt. To him, the mythical, the plastic and the tragic are manifestations of the same immorality and death – components of an All (83) that must be smashed like a false idol (Batnitzky 2000), a Greek marble statue. Through Walter Benjamin, this iconoclastic zeal will be transmitted to several theories, from the Frankfurt School to deconstruction and beyond.

The fundamental question for this generation is the place of humanity in a world whose historicity seems so inhospitable: 'How *does* man in all his solitude take his place in a world driven by spirit?' (83) The situation of the modern hero points to an interesting, counter-Aristotelian direction: 'What transpires on the stage does not advance him to fear and sympathy but rather to contradiction and involvement' (209). This is because his tragedy 'aims for a goal which is quite alien to classical tragedy: for a tragedy of the absolute man in his relationship to the absolute object' (210). Rosenzweig draws on Spengler and Kierkegaard to identify this man as Faust complemented by Don Juan, and to propose (contradicting his earlier claim about the irreducible variety of modern heroes) that all the unique modern heroes converge to 'this absolute human being who not only confronts the Absolute knowingly, but who has experienced the Absolute and who now, out of this experience, lives within the Absolute, this character whom the Faust-dramas can only strive for without attaining him because they remain, still and yet, stuck in the limited life – this is none other than the saint. The tragedy of the saint is the secret longing of the tragedian' (211). There is no need for Faustian character to mature towards catastrophe, like Spengler's Lear. All drama aspires to the mystery play.

However, this longing cannot be fulfilled because the saint, as a perfect human being, 'rules out the possibility of a tragedy which in essence is and remains a character-tragedy' (211). Modern tragedy yearns to reach beyond art and obliterate itself: instead of pursuing this unattainable goal of turning the saint into a hero, the tragic poet aches to become 'the servant of God' and take the position of a beloved soul which, opened and surrendered, 'vanished amorphously in the divine love. It threatened to dissolve in its mere prostration before God' (211). The title of book 3, where all this is announced, is explicit: 'Redemption, or The Eternal Future of the Kingdom'. The tragedy of irreversible time is overcome by Rosenzweig's narrative of creation, revelation and redemption.

In many respects, Rosenzweig's trajectory may be compared to that of near contemporaries like Lev Shestov (1866-1938). Although in his early *Dostoevsky and Nietzsche: The Philosophy of Tragedy* (1903) he explores in detail the tragic qualities of the two thinkers, Shestov soon concludes that evil, suffering and tragedy defy rational explanation, and he begins to preach the idea of unfounded faith as groundlessness, abyss, refusal, primordial freedom and violence. Attacking rationalism, positivism and 'the virus of European culture and ethics', he launches a life-long attack on Socrates ('the Adam of philosophy') and Spinoza (his 'second incarnation'), defending Abraham who knew how to live in uncertainty. To him, and likewise to Rosenzweig, 'Athens' means constraining speculative thought, invented truth and sinful metaphysics, while 'Jerusalem' signifies free biblical thought, eternal truth and biblical epistemology (Shestov 1966). Before the end of the second decade of the twentieth century, knowledge and history, on the one hand, and faith and revelation, on the other, emerge as rival worldviews.

Walter Benjamin (1928)

> [T]he modern theatre has nothing to show which remotely resembles the tragedy of the Greeks. In denying this actual state of affairs ... doctrines of the tragic betray the presumption that it must still be possible to write tragedies.
>
> Benjamin 1977: 101

When Walter Benjamin (1892-1940) begins in 1924 to write his 'Habilitation' thesis, *The Origin of the German Trauerspiel/ Mourning-Play* (1928), he has already been preoccupied with the philosophy of tragedy for almost ten years. In the thesis, he dismisses the entire theory of tragedy created by German Idealism and seeks to replace it with 'the philosophy of the history of tragedy' (Szondi 2002: 49). He objects to the universalism and the moralism of Idealist approaches, like Johannes Volkelt's recent *Ästhetik des Tragischen* (1917), which argue that tragedy offers edifying lessons to all humanity. Rejecting figurative 'cheap reflection' (Benjamin 1977: 105), he focuses on mimesis itself. Art can neither give moral counsel to conscience nor permit the object of representation to be the object of attention. The truth content of its totality is manifest only in 'the critical elaboration of the work itself' (105). In order to observe the prohibition against graven images, art must concentrate attention on representation itself, and so must the study of tragedy (105).

While Lukács locates the ethics of tragedy in its form, Benjamin attempts to move beyond figurative reflections, studying the (profane) mimetic function as deterioration of the pure, primordial language of meaning. Consistently, he turns Lukács's historico-philo-sophical approach into an aesthetico-theological hermeneutics, a tendency noted by his contemporaries. Commenting in 1928 on the *Trauerspiel* book and *One Way Street*, both of which had come out this same year, Siegfried Kracauer notes that 'the two works belong together as expressions of a type of thinking that is foreign to current thought. Such thinking is more akin to talmudic writings and

125

medieval tractates, for, like these, its manner of presentation [*Darstellungsform*] is interpretation. Its intentions are of a theological sort' (Kracauer 1995: 259).

Benjamin elaborates a theory of tragic presentation of legend on the basis of a three-stage development: fate, sacrifice, atonement (Wolin 1980: 77). He sees in tragedy a unique struggle of humanity against fate, against the mythical justice of the Olympians. The ancient rights of the Olympian gods destroy the hero because these rights do not measure up to the demands of his or her tragic will but at the same time the fate of this hero prefigures the future of his or her community. His death transcends the confines of old myth and redeems the collectivity, an achievement which belongs to that future community. All this is part of *agon*, the contest in which all ancient plays participate and which in turn provides their basic structure. The performance of the tragic hero, the sacrificial victim, in the *agon* is defined by his silence. Here Benjamin adopts Rosenzweig's definition of the 'meta-ethical man' (Benjamin 1977: 107-8), the actual 'self' of the pagan man who wills his individuality without relying on any outside norms, and remains speechless because he no longer communicates with the world of gods or fellow men. Rosenzweig contrasts to the classical tragedy of paganism revelation in which man emerges from the mute isolation of elemental self-assertion and enters a relationship with God and Man.

Benjamin had already adopted Rosenzweig's idea of the speechless hero in his essay 'Fate and Character' (1921). There he argued that the tragic hero breaches demonic fate and liberates himself from the 'endless pagan chain of guilt and atonement' (1978: 307). But that does not mean he gains his innocence or achieves purity. 'Rather, in tragedy pagan man becomes aware that he is better than his god, but the realization robs him of speech, remains unspoken. ... The paradox of the birth of genius in moral speechlessness, moral infantility, is the sublimity of tragedy' (307). In the *Trauerspiel* book too, Benjamin equates silence with Lukácsian selfhood. The hero is caught between the legal language of the ancient statutes, which in the end destroy him, and the yet uncreated language of a distant community. 'In the presence of the suffering hero the community learns reverence and gratitude for the word with which his death endowed it – a word which shone out in another place as a new gift

126

whenever the poet extracted some new meaning from the legend' (1977: 109). The achievement of speechlessness is that, by rejecting the traditional principles of justification altogether, it 'throws suspicion back onto his persecutors. For its meaning is inverted: what appears before the public is not the guilt of the accused but the evidence of speechless suffering, and the tragedy which appeared to be devoted to the judgment of the hero is transformed into a hearing about the Olympians' (109) and a proclamation of 'the anti-Olympian prophecy of all tragic poetry' (109).

The tragic hero, by sacrificing himself to the Olympian fate, opens the way for a future ethical community but his own ethic is neither conscious nor articulate. He is a one-dimensional, soulless creature who is always the same self, always sentenced, always dumb, always dead – rooted and buried in his self. Although defiant, he resigns himself to speechlessness since he cannot overcome myth. This is the tyranny of mythical fate which annihilates those who challenge it. Unable to make law or history, he is destined to be another innocent victim in the ritual cycle of the sacrificial agon. Benjamin understands this *agon* in terms of his three-stage narrative of hubris/fate, punishment/sacrifice, and redemption/atonement. The silent hero is aware of this contract:

> Only antiquity could know tragic *hubris*, which pays for the right to be silent with the hero's life. The hero, who scorns to justify himself before the gods, reaches agreement with them in a, so to speak, contractual process of atonement which, in its dual significance, is designed not only to bring about the restoration but above all the undermining of an ancient body of laws in the linguistic constitution of the renewed community. Athletic contests, law, and tragedy constitute the great agonal trinity of Greek life ... and they are bound together under the sign of this contract.
>
> Benjamin 1977: 115

At this point, Benjamin's concept of the tragic as the helpless speechlessness of the hero begins to break down as he introduces parallels between trial and tragedy. If tragedy is understood in terms of trial proceedings, rather than religious ritual, the presence of a silent victim becomes meaningless, as the power of free speech makes itself heard:

> The important and characteristic feature of Athenian law is the Dionysian outburst, the fact that the intoxicated, ecstatic word was able to transcend the regular perimeter of the *agon*, that a higher justice was vouchsafed by the persuasive power of living speech than from the trial of the opposed factions, by combat with weapons or prescribed verbal forms. The practice of the trial by ordeal is disrupted by the freedom of the *logos*. This is the ultimate affinity between trial and tragedy in Athens.
>
> Benjamin 1977: 116

What is happening on the stage is not a ceremony but an unpredictable negotiation which follows the rules of a procedure, not the norms of a custom, and deals with injured parties, witnesses and prosecutors, rather than sacrificial victims, gods, and priests. 'The community is present at this re-opening of the proceedings as the controlling, indeed as the adjudicating authority. For its part it seeks to reach a decision about the settlement, in the interpretation of which the dramatist renews the memory of the achievements of the hero' (116). This is the 'forensic dramaturgy of tragedy' (117) taking place before the 'adjudicating assembly of the populace' (116). It is not searching for either absolute right or redemption. It is a negotiation aiming at the higher justice of conciliation. It is a contest whose participants, its heroes, do not 'speak' precisely because they debate, through dialogue, the validity of existing laws, settlements and traditions. Thus Benjamin seems to oscillate between silence and performance, between the analogies of the sacrifice and the courtroom.

Like Rosenzweig before him, Benjamin rejects the idea that a rejuvenation of tragedy is possible. The Greek past represents the only possibility of tragedy. 'Whereas Nietzsche's *Birth of Tragedy* seemed to establish a theory of modernity as a scenario of tragedy, Benjamin's book on the *Trauerspiel* proposes a theory of modernity as a theory of the *Trauerspiel* in radical opposition to tragedy. The incompatibility of tragedy and *Trauerspiel* is the architectural foundation' (Nägele 1991: 113) of the latter treatise. In the early twentieth century, artists, writers, critics and philosophers embrace

128

Nietzsche's call for a rejuvenation of tragedy through a recovery of its origins. Benjamin is determined to discredit this effort: his God did not die – he only forsook the world. 'An incomplete secularization, the indirect yield of Lutheranism, had left the world with a vacuum from which tragic freedom and tragic grandeur could no longer emerge. The theatre of this vacuum, its ennui, its irrational and cruel passions, is that of *deus absconditus*, the theater of the hidden god' (Heller 1991: 311). Caught between nostalgia and anticipation, Benjamin and other people of his generation aimed to give the godforsaken world of modernity an alternative, messianic vision, with the 'angel of history' providing hope, utopia and redemption. It all hinges on the conviction that the historical predicament is melancholic, not tragic, as mortals look forward to Judgment Day. As Benjamin argued in 1916, the universality of the *Trauerspiel* is no longer mythic and not yet historical but a hybrid of the two – it is spectral. Since its time is finite and yet not fulfilled, non-individual and yet without the certitude of higher existence, it has no conclusive finality. If tragic time is only individually fulfilled, true historical time (the time of the empirical event) is infinite and unfulfilled. Fulfilled historical time is not individually fulfilled; it is messianic time, the historical idea provided by the Bible (Benjamin 1996: 55-6).

When Lukács realizes that his ethical concerns have disappeared in Benjamin's aesthetic approach to drama, he criticizes the *Trauerspiel* book for irrationalism and decadence. It is too late, though, as members of the Frankfurt School adopt Benjamin as their Socrates, and turn his life into a modernist martyr play.

Joseph Wood Krutch (1929)

We read but we do not write tragedies. The tragic solution of the problem of existence, the reconciliation to life by means of the tragic spirit is, that is to say, now only a fiction surviving in art. When that art itself has become, as it probably will, completely meaningless, when we have ceased not only to write but to *read* tragic works, then it will be lost and in all real senses forgotten, since the devolution from Religion to Art to Document will be complete.

Krutch 1929: 142-3

The Spenglerian vision of Joseph Wood Krutch (1893-1970) allows for no redemptive anticipation. In the chapter 'The Tragic Fallacy' of his book *The Modern Temper* (1929), Krutch insists that tragedy appears when a people muster enough fortitude in the face of disaster to become confident in man's greatness. Thus it expresses triumph over despair, and faith in life. To be sure, this is a tragic faith because it gives dignity to those who share the illusion that the events of the world and the desires of the heart correspond to one another. Tragic faith is nourished by the tragic fallacy of a people that behind life's dissonances they can hear a cosmic harmony.

Today this tragic solution to the riddles of existence is no longer available. After Nietzsche, nobody can offer a tragic justification because Moderns may experience pathos but not nobility, dignity or elation. People are out of joint with their world and do not attribute to their actions any large significance. With the ensuing weakening of confidence and enfeeblement of spirit, we can no longer write tragedies, no matter how much we need them, no matter how much we still talk about the tragic spirit. What is more, the death of tragedy prefigures the end of all art and the dominance of a mean life in a meaningless universe, deprived of the consolations of the tragic fallacy.

Other writers reach less apocalyptic conclusions. In his essay 'Tragedy and the Whole Truth' (1931), Aldous Huxley (1894-1963) writes that, even though tragedy 'happens to be passing through a period of eclipse, ... there is no good reason to believe that this state of things will last forever. Tragedy is too valuable to be allowed to die' (Huxley 1980: 156-7). The same year, Kenneth Burke (1897-1993), who differentiates between tragic drama and tragic spirit, grants the death of the former but hails the survival of the latter in Krutch's own moral stability and calamitous persistence against the current historical process (Burke 1931: 252-5). Fifteen years later Jean-Paul Sartre (1905-80) outlines in his New York lecture, 'Forgers of Myths: The Young Playwrights of France' (Sartre 1976), the rejuvenation of tragedy on the stage in a form that rejects symbols in favour of myths as it draws confidently on ancient and neo-classical, philosophical and psychological, historical and ceremonial resources. Like fellow writers Jean Giraudoux and Albert Camus, Sartre is very confident about the living presence of tragedy in France. The place of tragedy in the United States, however, has always elicited rather extreme views. Some find it highly promising: 'Of all peoples of the world, we hunger most deeply for tragedy; and perhaps in America alone the emergence of a tragic literature is still possible. ... In Western Europe, the tragic tension no longer exists; it is too easy to despair and to fall in love with one's despair. Melodrama, *comédie larmoyante*, learned irony and serious parody – these are the forms proper to the contemporary European mind. In the orbit of Stalinism, on the other hand, despair has been legislated away' (Fiedler 1952: 297). Other critics believe that the American worldview has no room for tragic understanding because of its optimism, naturalism, opportunism, interest in the ordinary person, and fascination with distracting social types, such as the victim and the villain (Klapp 1958).

Nikolai Berdyaev (1931)

> The good is realized through contradictions, sacrifices and suffering. The good is paradoxical. The moral life is tragic, for the very appearance of the distinction between good and evil was a terrible tragedy.
>
> Berdyaev 1960: 160

Nicolas Berdyaev continues the Russian tradition of ethical inquiry into the tragic, bringing it closer to an Orthodox approach. In *The Destiny of Man* (1931) he argues that, since sacrifice always indicates tragedy, it is impossible to deny tragedy in Christ, the God of sacrificial love. Tragedy represents the manifestation of the 'inner dramatism of the Divine life' (29). Tragic conflict in the life of the Deity is a sign of perfection, not inadequacy. Already the creation of the world requires movement in God and constitutes a dramatic event (rather than serene self-sufficiency). Like all tragedy, the tragedy of God is connected with freedom, his freedom to sacrifice himself for humanity so that he can share his creatures' destiny and help them reconcile themselves to the tragedy of the world (30).

There are two kinds of tragedy, those of fate and freedom. 'Pre-Christian tragedy is the hopeless misery and suffering of the innocent. It is the tragedy of fate. It is based upon the interpretation of cosmic life as completely self-contained. There is no supercosmic God to whom the innocent sufferer can appeal. ... The only way out is through aesthetic reconciliation, through feeling the beauty of hopeless suffering' (31). The essence of tragedy, the tragic as such, emerges in the Christian tragedy of freedom, which reveals tragedy in the Divine life itself as the Only Begotten Son, an innocent sufferer, is crucified. This revelation shows the deeper struggle between opposites 'when two equally divine principles come into conflict. ... The greatest tragedy is suffering caused by the good and not by evil, and consists in our being unable to justify life in terms of the distinction between good and evil' (31-2). Pure tragedy presupposes freedom of choice, and

132

consists in the conflict of lofty values. Therefore, rather than another German 'epistemological justification' (1), we need a new ethics which will incorporate 'knowledge not only of good and evil, but also of the tragic which is constantly present in moral experience and complicates all our moral judgments. The paradoxicality of moral life is connected with the presence in it of the tragic element which cannot be subsumed under the ordinary categories of good and evil. The tragic is not a result of evil but is morally guiltless' (32). Tragic conflicts can be solved only when creative freedom broadens the moral domain by violating law and norm. Beyond the morality of good and bad, of divine and diabolical, lies the supreme tragedy of the innocent Crucified, the tragedy of the cross, which overcomes the tragedy of freedom.

In the essay 'Christianity and Tragedy' of his book *Beyond Tragedy* (1938), Reinhold Niebuhr (1892-1971) rejects this approach: 'Jesus is, superficially considered, a tragic figure; yet not really so. Christianity is a religion which transcends tragedy. ... The cross is not tragic but the resolution of tragedy' (Niebuhr 1938: 155). In general, the place of tragedy in monotheism has attracted a broad variety of views. W.H. Auden (1907-73) supports it in a study of Melville's Captain Ahab where he distinguishes between the flaw of hubris in the Greek tragedy of necessity (Berdyaev's fate), and the sin of pride in the Christian tragedy of possibility (Berdyaev's freedom) (Auden 1967: 40-1). In contrast, Karl Jaspers (1883-1969) insists that, since 'Christian salvation opposes tragic knowledge ... no genuinely Christian tragedy can exist' (Jaspers 1969: 38). Regarding the Hebrew Bible, some believe that, because relativity of values and pluralism of truths are the clearest mark of the tragic situation, the 'Biblical narrative by itself ... lacks all elements required by the world of tragedy' (Kurzweil 1966: 111); while others hold that, although it is incompatible with Christianity, 'tragedy can get a start in a religious vision of human life, and of the cosmos, which is "Jewish" or Manichean' (Michel 1956: 428). In most of these explorations, philosophical issues yield to questions of faith and dogma combined with genre and comparative philology. They might be evaluated with this remark by George Santayana (1863-1952) in mind: 'I can think of only one tragedy in which religion might well play a leading part, and that is the tragedy of religion itself' (Santayana 1936: 375).

Martin Heidegger (1935)

The strangest (man) is what it is because, fundamentally, it cultivates and guards the familiar, only in order to break out of it and to let what overpowers it break in. Being itself hurls man into this breaking-away, which drives him beyond himself to venture forth toward being, to accomplish being, to stabilize it in the work, and so hold open the essent as a whole.

Heidegger 1959: 163

In order to elucidate Parmenides' definition of being-human, Martin Heidegger (1889-1976) undertakes in his *Introduction to Metaphysics* (1935) an interpretation of the first choral ode in Sophocles' *Antigone*, where man is called the superlative *deinotaton* of all things. According to this close reading, the adjective *deinos*/awesome means both 'terrible' (referring to power as perceived potentiality) and 'powerful' (referring to power as realized manifestation). This word, which describes the essent as a whole, 'has the strange ambiguity with which Greek discourse cuts across the contending separations [*Aus-einander-setzungen*] of being' (149). Sophocles calls man the most *deinon* thing, first, because he belongs by his essence to the *deinon* and remains exposed to its overpowering power, and, second, because he gathers the power violently and brings it to manifestation. This link and limit of man's being make him *deinotaton*/strange and uncanny, the strangest of all, in that he departs violently from customary limits, he breaks the limits of the familiar.

Heidegger calls the powerful quality of the violent man *techne*/art, which he takes to mean transgressive knowledge, and the natural order (the object of man's violent knowing) *dike*/justice, which he takes to signify the governing structure. *Techne* means the historical man's being-there, while *dike* denotes the presence of essent as a whole. The *deinon* as violence collects its essence in *techne* while the *deinon* as overpowering is manifested in *dike* (160). 'The *deinotaton*

134

of the *deinon*, the strangest of the strange, lies in the conflict between *dike* and *techne'* (162).

Because he embodies the actuality of violence and the potentiality of power, man is profoundly contradictory in that his essence (his natural limits) is to violate (his limits), his nature is to transgress his nature. This inherent contradiction endows him with a tragic destiny whose 'ultimate' fulfilment also represents 'abysmal' (149) catastrophe. The two related but contrary forces are destined to clash in man when 'the *deinon* as overpowering (*dike*) and the *deinon* as the violent (*techne*) confront one another, though not as two given things. In this confrontation *techne* bursts forth against *dike*, which in turn, as Fug, the commanding order, disposes [*verfügt*] of all *techne'* (160-1). Man cultivates the familiar only in order to break out of it. When that occurs, 'the assault of *techne* against *dike* is the happening whereby man ceases to be at home. ... Through the event of homelessness the whole of the essent is disclosed' (167). Like a tragic hero, man believes that his crafty *techne*/violent knowledge can give him mastery over cosmic *dike*/overpowering order without realizing that his activity draws its power from the governing structure of the world. 'The violence of poetic speech, of thinking projection, of building configuration, of the action that creates states is not a function of faculties that man has, but a taming and ordering of powers by virtue of which the essent opens up as such when man moves into it. This disclosure of the essent is the power that man must master in order to become himself amid the essent, i.e. in order to be historical' (157).

The human tragedy is that 'the violent act [*Gewalt-tat*] of laying out paths into the environing power of the essent' (157) may bring disaster as man breaks out and breaks up, 'captures and subjugates' (157). At the same time, it also signals the triumph of *dike* since man's transgressive entry into history discloses its supreme power. Parmenides' claim about the bond between *noein*/apprehension and *einai*/being confirms the same principle (165) – the reciprocal relation between the two meanings of *deinon*, between knowledge and order. In his historical ruin, man the *deinotaton*/strangest consummates the active pursuit of knowledge and, by suffering for it, discloses his struggle against order to be part of that cosmic order.

Discussing the Anaximander fragment eleven years later, in 1946, Heidegger argues that *didonai diken tes adikias* means the same thing: the presencing of whatever is present for the time being, what-ever lingers awhile, consists in disorder as well as in letting its essence as presencing belong to order, to the non-present, by surmounting disorder. 'The experience of beings in their Being which here comes to language is neither pessimistic nor nihilistic; nor is it optimistic. It is tragic' (1975: 44). Beings, which linger awhile in presence, become present, first, when they cling to themselves, hang on, strike a haughty pose, aim at everlasting continuance, and stand in disorder, ignoring the lingering presence of others and the order of the while; and at the same time when they let belong, one to the another, when they grant heed and esteem to one another in their conjoining order. 'If what is present grants order, it happens in this manner: as beings linger awhile, they give *Ruch*/reck to one another. The surmounting of disorder properly occurs through the letting-belong of reck' (47). Tragic order prevails over recklessness. '*In* our tragic loss of coming to be passing away – in our obsession with presence in lingering for a while – Heidegger finds the hope of *to khreon* [necessity]: our insistent presence is nonetheless let be. ... We belong both to the hinge of pres-ence and to the unhinging of presence. Without a sense of stability of the securing bounds of a determinate origin, we have found an insep-arability of the tragic and hope, a strange joining of catastrophe and vitality whose measure is traced but not fully thought in the heritage that gives us to think and speak' (Scott 1996: 66).

A historicist explanation of this theory can claim that the tragic thematic appears in 1934-5 at the moment of Heidegger's retreat from politics, 'that is to say the moment of disappointment with respect to Nazism' (Lacoue-Labarthe and Nancy 1997: 79). A different explanation might place it in the history of philosophy and connect it with the emergence of the tragic problematic in the 1790s. Heidegger himself attempted such a connection a few years earlier, when he studied at length the meaning of Kantian autonomy.

In a 1930 lecture course at Freiburg, 'An Introduction to Philosophy', Heidegger emphasizes that freedom does not need to be conceived primarily in terms of causality. Several other perspectives on freedom are possible. But since Kant was the first to see the ques-tion of freedom in its most radical dimension, Heidegger keeps this question within the Kantian perspective of causality in order to establish a dialogue with his predecessor while at the same time

rejecting Neo-Kantianism (Langiulli 1971: 190-203). More important, he continues, is to reposition freedom so that the question of its
essence is not built into the leading problem of philosophy but, on the
contrary, freedom emerges as something prior even to being and time
that grounds the possibility of Dasein.

> Freedom is not some particular thing among and alongside
> other things, but is superordinate and governing in relation to
> the whole. But if we are seeking out freedom as the ground of
> the possibility of existence, then freedom must itself, in its
> essence, be more primordial than man. Man is only an adminis-
> trator of freedom, i.e. he can only let-be the freedom which is
> accorded to him, in such a way that, through man, the whole
> contingency of freedom becomes visible. Human freedom now
> no longer means freedom as the property of man, but man as a
> possibility of freedom. Human freedom is the freedom that
> breaks through in man and takes him up unto itself, thus
> making man possible. If freedom is the ground of the possibility
> of existence, the root of being and time, and thus the ground of
> the possibility of understanding being in its while breadth and
> fullness, then man, as grounded in his existence upon and in
> this freedom, is the site where beings in the whole become
> revealed, i.e. he is that particular being through which beings as
> such announce themselves.
>
> Heidegger 2002: 93-4

Heidegger recovers from man's existential uniqueness the metaphysical greatness of his essence grounded in the freedom of his
existence, namely, the greatness of finitude (rather than deceptive
infinity). Seen from his essence grounded in freedom, man appears as
the awesome being in whom the being of beings is revealed; the
remarkable being in whose fundamental ground the understanding
of being occurs; the glorious being that 'can only be as the most finite
of all beings, as the convergence of opposing elements within the
sphere of beings, and thus as the *occasion and possibility of the separation* of beings in their *diversity*' (94).

Heidegger argues that freedom is neither a psychological concept
(belonging to the will) nor a theological principle (belonging to God)

but rather a cosmological idea belonging to the world as totality of present beings accessible to human knowledge (144). Thus freedom is not opposed to natural causality but, as a problem arising from the world and as the problem of the world, a distinct mode of that causality. Specifically, freedom is absolute natural causality (148), an idea of nature that transcends all possible experience, raising the concept of nature to the absolutely unconditioned (through which the conditioned has been possible). The concept of causality is the concept that the idea of transcendental freedom represents. Cosmological freedom is the transcendental idea of unconditioned causality (177). But by raising nature to the unconditioned, it brings to light a conflict between doctrine and counter-doctrine within reason which Kant treated as the third antinomy – the antinomy in reason's understanding of the unconditioned totality or causal conditionedness of beings.

Heidegger takes a metaphysical approach to the question's rootedness in human nature in an attempt to unite unconditioned causality (causality from freedom) and natural causality. While the antinomy of freedom appears as a cosmological antagonism, he argues that, when the thesis posits nature as finite (since causality comes from freedom) and the antithesis as infinite, both rest on a false presupposition, that of nature as a thing-in-itself. 'This presupposition overlooks the fact that as the fundamental concept of appearance, nature cannot possess absolute existence. Since nature is not being-in-itself it cannot be said to be either finite or infinite' (161). Thus the Kantian antagonism is revealed to be a mere dialectical opposition (rather than a contradiction) and can be removed. There is no need to place the truth on either side, to decide between freedom and nature. Taking appearances as things-in-themselves is an illusion necessary to common reason but essentially it expresses a distinction between finite and infinite knowledge. 'The problem of pure reason must therefore be recognized as the problem of finite knowledge' (161).

In order to give a positive resolution to the inner antagonism of reason, philosophy must uncover the unity of its opposing sides, causality from freedom and natural causality, and show that a world event may be determined by both. For Kant, the problem cannot be resolved at a general ontological level but only discussed in terms of an application to a particular being, '*man as ethically acting person*' (166). 'The elucidation of the universal metaphysical construction of the possible unity of nature and freedom shows that there is indeed a world-entity in which this unity factically exists, i.e. in man as a rational living being' (176). Thus freedom as a causality of reason can be saved in the face of natural necessity.

Ultimately Heidegger reverses the metaphysical categories: 'If *causality is a problem of freedom* and not vice versa then the *problem of being in general* is in itself a *problem of freedom*. However, the problem of being ... is the fundamental problem of philosophy as such. Thus *the question concerning the essence of human freedom is the fundamental question of philosophy, in which is rooted even the question of being*' (203). What started as an exploration of the possibility of freedom according to the Kantian approach through causality concludes that causality is grounded in freedom. '*Freedom is the condition of the possibility of the manifestness of the being of beings, of the understanding of being. ...* If actual being-free and willing from the ground of essence determines the fundamental philosophical stance, and thus the content of philosophy' (205), then philosophy must, as Kant first instructed, give its laws unto itself, rejecting heteronomous advances or commands.

A few years later, Heidegger reads the Kantian problematic in the framework of the *Antigone*, and discovers that the unity of nature and freedom can be contradictory, leading to a clash between order and knowledge, violation of cosmic justice, and the endowment of humans with tragic destiny. In the *Introduction*, freedom as expressed by humans standing in disorder continues to be the condition of possibility of the emergence of conjoining order. However the validity of self-legislation, and the legitimacy of self-institution, are issues that have disappeared completely from the horizon.

Epilogue

After Heidegger, German thinkers more or less abandon tragic reflection. Rare exceptions like Ernst Bloch and Carl Schmitt belong to Heidegger's generation. Karl Jaspers and Hannah Arendt realize early on that the topic has lost its centrality for their culture. An empirical account of this exhaustion based on the horrors of World War Two, which presumably made tragedy redundant, would be inadequate. The defeat of tragic thought follows the onslaught against myth in the 1920s. The German paradox of this thought is that dialectics, which was the main effort of coming to terms with the antinomy of liberty, treats the conflict between freedom and necessity as a matter of aesthetic, rather than political, autonomy, of individual self-determination rather than collective self-governance, and so practises opposition as *Kulturkritik*. By the Weimar era, this critique is so self-satisfied with its aesthetic purity and moral superiority that it abandons all tragic responsibility, blaming instead the modern predicament on myth.

While approaching its point of decline in Germany, the tragic idea migrates to France, together with a new Hegelianism of the *Phenomenology*. Beginning with Jean Wahl's *The Unhappy Consciousness in Hegel's Philosophy* (1929), the tragic makes its presence felt in a continuous line of thinkers that includes Alexandre Kojève, Jean Hyppolite, Lucien Goldmann, Gabriel Marcel, Jean-Paul Sartre, Albert Camus, Roland Barthes, Jacques Lacan, Maurice Blanchot, Paul Ricoeur, René Girard, Edgar Marin, Gilles Deleuze, Kostas Papaioannou, Jacques Derrida and Hélène Cixous. This theoretical elaboration coincides with both the writing of new tragedies and the intense interest among directors from Antonin Artaud to Ariane Mnouchkine. Thus it establishes itself as an integral part of French culture.

There has been an equally diverse growth of British attention, including the Cambridge Ritualists, George Thomson, Raymond Williams, Iris Murdoch, George Steiner, the New Historicists (with their special interest in the Renaissance and the Baroque), Ruth Padel, Edith Hall and numerous other researchers interested in classical reception. The King's College London 1993 conference on 'Tragedy and "The Tragic"' (Silk 1996), the Archive of Performance of Greek and Roman Drama (1996) at the University of Oxford, the Centre for the Classical Tradition (early 1990s) at the University of Bristol and the faculty consortium Contexts for Classics (2000) at the University of Michigan are a few institutional landmarks of this growth. Near the end of the twentieth century the trend converges with the creative work of playwrights Tony Harrison, Edward Bond and Howard Barker, director Peter Hall and actress Fiona Shaw. The parallel American tradition, which dates to the 1920s, includes Eva Palmer-Sikelianos, Kenneth Burke, George Santayana, Francis Ferguson, Susanne Langer, Richard Sewall, Walter Kaufmann, Elder Olson, Lionel Abel, Morse Peckham, Gerald Else and Murray Krieger, along with corresponding numbers of playwrights and directors. Indeed, the list of non-German writers who have made philosophical or broadly theoretical contributions to the study of the tragic at the turn of the twenty-first century is remarkable: John Anton, Judith Butler, Cornelius Castoriadis, Stanley Cavell, Terry Eagleton, Peter Euben, Simon Goldhill, Stanley Hauerwas, Philip Lacoue-Labarthe, Nicole Loraux, Martha Nussbaum, Timothy Reiss, John Sallis, Arlene Saxonhouse, George Steiner, Jean-Paul Vernant, Bernard Williams, Slavoj Žižek. No less impressive is the list of names representing anthropological approaches to the same idea.

Even a brief survey like this, which is narrowly focused on a few writers and countries, is enough to indicate that the question of the tragic continues to attract interest from thinkers from widely diverse backgrounds and with varying ideological commitments, who feel that this conversation is not any particular school's or discipline's prerogative. The tragic idea turns tragedy from an object to a problem that can be approached from several directions such as ethics, aesthetics, criticism, political theory, anthropology, psychology, psychoanalysis, study of myth and of ritual, women's studies, religious studies and theatre studies.

The epoch-making system of truth sanctioned by tragic understanding worked gloriously for about two centuries under the aegis of dialectics. However, under the pressures of post-structuralist critique, the intimate link between dialectics and the tragic is broken when antinomies are embraced as part of the human condition, and the utopian vision of totality is abandoned. Such a dramatic development gives a new direction to the question of the possibility of tragedy. This question, which has accompanied the tragic idea since its inception, loses its universal character and becomes localized and temporalized. Here are some of its better-known postmodern forms.

1. Is the tragic possible only in certain cultures? Some commentators claim that American popular culture lacks a tragic dimension, and consequently cannot comprehend properly calamities such as September 11, while others compare presidents like Kennedy, Nixon and Clinton to figures like Richard III, Oedipus and Lear. The legitimacy of the tragic within the non-Western world has been also debated among scholars and authors like Robert Plant Armstrong, P.J. Conradie, Ato Quayson and Wole Soyinka.

2. Is the tragic possible within monotheism? Jewish and Christian theologians and religious thinkers continue to support a wide range of positions, with journals of theological and biblical journals devoting their pages to possible connections between Abrahamic hope and idolatrous despair.

3. Is the tragic possible within Marxism? Herbert Weisinger argues in 1963 that deterministic Marxism, an inheritor of Humanism with strong mythological/religious elements, can inspire tragedy if approached with an attitude of sceptical faith. George Szanto declares in 1983 that tragedy and the tragic are out of place in the modern world, which demands economic and political modes of thought. Ernst Schumacher insists in 1990 that Marxists still opt for 'detragicizing history' despite 'internal tragedies' within progressive movements.

4. Is the tragic compatible with psychoanalysis? Since Jacques Lacan gave the tragic a prominent position, writers who have explored its proper place include André Green, Luce Irigaray, Soshana Felman, Stathis Gourgouris, Judith Butler, Slavoj Zizek, Yannis Stavrakakis and Olga Taxidou.

5. Does the tragic remain available after a certain era (Classical Greece, Baroque Spain, Humanist Germany) and author (Euripides,

Racine, Ibsen, Freud), or during a modern condition, such as autonomy (Barker 1993: 104), capitalism (Zizek 2001: 102), colonialism (Reiss 2002: 109) and the hermeneutic of trial (Soni, forthcoming)? Regarding specifically the Greeks, some insist that we are entirely different from them (Steiner), while others find that we are crucially similar: 'We are in an ethical condition that lies not only beyond Christianity, but beyond its Kantian and its Hegelian legacies. ... We know that the world was not made for us, or we for the world, that our history tells no purposive story, and that there is no position outside the world or outside history from which we might hope to authenticate our activities. ... In important ways, we are, in our ethical situation, more like human beings in antiquity than any Western people have been in the meantime' (Williams 1993: 166).

6. Does the tragic inhere in specific domains? Many focus on specific issues or areas which they consider by nature tragic: war (military historian Victor Davis Hanson), international relations (political theorist Richard Ned Lebow), being human (political theorist Michael Dillon), the hermeneutical experience (literary theorist Gerald Bruns), allocation choices (public policy specialists Guido Calabresi and Philip Bobbitt), the medical profession (theologian Stanley Hauerwas) or narratives in supermarket tabloids (popular culture specialist Richard Keller Simon).

7. Is the tragic compatible with an explicitly political theatre? In the 1970s, Heiner Müller and Augusto Boal reject conventional theatre and value process over product, though they take different approaches to tragedy depending on their commitment to the revolution. Others have concluded that it is not a question of what kind of drama is needed (for example, political or not) but whether drama is at all possible, complaining that

the present-day theatre presents two aspects, on the one hand a museum, but on the other a field for experiments, so much so that every play presents the author with new tasks, new questions of style. Today style is no longer anything general, but something personal, indeed, it has been a matter for decision from one case to another. ... If now there are only styles, there are now only dramatic theories and there is no longer any dramatic theory.

Dürrenmatt 1976: 67

In a world where the state is thoroughly bureaucratic, academic study prevails over art, the audience understands itself as victims, heroes are nameless, parody creeps into all genres, and writers are only confused grandchildren, literature may be studied but not created.

8. Is the tragic meaningful when the stage has been rendered redundant by postmodern performative practices (such as parodying, passing, mimicking, staging, gender/race bending and carnivalling) which have prevailed in the public domain? Theories of figural theatre describing the dramatic conditions of social life converge with theories of ritual performance describing revisionary adaptations of staged identity. An overwhelming list of names comes to mind: playwright Nicolas Evreinoff, literary scholar Kenneth Burke, sociologists Erving Goffman and Georges Gurvitch, historian Johan Huizinga, semiotician Juri Lotman, phenomenologist Bruce Wilshire, social historian Richard Sennett, director Richard Schechner, feminist Marilyn Frye, anthropologists Clifford Geertz and Victor Turner, literary critic Richard Poirier, art critic Harold Rosenberg, art historian Michael Fried, political theorists Tracy Strong and Thomas Meier, psychologist Karl Scheibe, cultural studies specialist Timothy Murray, theatre theorists Peggy Phelan and Philip Auslander, gender theorists Eve Kosofsky Sedgwick and Judith Butler, and post-colonial scholar Homi Bhabha. 'Society ... can be viewed as a constant performance, a kind of ever-present aestheticized metatheater, that forces all people as role-players into the roles, ironically, of perpetual spectators, evaluating the performances of themselves and others' (Richards 1991: xv). As the 1990s dramatic model of understanding succeeded the 1970s textual one, as performative approaches replaced interpretive ones, and as self-fashioning took over minority identity, the primacy of theatricality in both creative and analytical engagements became pronounced. To supporters, this signals the dissolution of essentialism on the most basic personal level. To critics, the dissolution of politics by postmodern culturalism signals the ultimate triumph of *Kulturkritik* whereby form prevails over reason, and aesthetics over ethics (Mulhern 2000) as, according to the logic of the failed revolt, transgressive art form displaces the revolution (Starr 1995). Certain reasons can be invoked for calling the postmodern era post-tragic: tragedy is now

144

a closed genre, references to religious and mythical views no longer obtain, historical traumas have eclipsed the tragic experience, terrible beauty has been assimilated by the sublime. On the other hand, it has been counter-argued that '"tragedy" and "the tragic" have always been belated categories. The "tragic" is, and always was, a "post"-category of experience, discovered in interpretation. Likewise, the forms of literary-dramatic "tragedy" are and always were themselves post-tragic' (Bouchard 2001: 30).

9. Is tragic insight better expressed by non-theatrical arts? The trend towards performativity can be judged differently if placed in the context of numerous attempts in all the arts to create a modern tragedy or to surpass tragedy altogether by establishing a new tragic genre or form. The autonomization of the tragic has enabled tragedy to migrate through several genres, from novel to film to celebrity gossip. On the stage itself, if tragedy is followed first by anti-tragedy, and later by post-tragedy (Faas 1984: 24), then, instead of lamenting the 'death of tragedy', it might be more appropriate to celebrate the unique modern genre of metatheatre, where characters participate in their own dramatization (Abel 1963). Regarding fiction, Sidney Zink proposed in 1958 that the modern medium of tragedy is the novel, and the man of disbelief its tragic hero, while Murray Krieger argued in 1979 that the novel has deconstructed all drama, unless of course we grant that drama always self-deconstructs, mocking 'itself internally through being essentially, in its own way, a broken whole' (Murdoch 1993: 116). More broadly, it has been suggested that tragedy is neither a genre nor a worldview but rather a pattern of literary action embodied in various genres (Lenson 1975: 169).

10. Assuming it is true, what can be learned from the fact that the rise of the tragic idea coincided with the decline of tragedy? Timothy Reiss criticizes the 'hypostatization of the tragic', which has extracted out of tragedy a unique essence, and argues that

> when this transference of the discursive to a separate reality has been achieved then there is no more *need* for tragedy: the 'impossibility' that discourse had confronted of making meaning has been named as a knowable condition within an overall ordering of the real. It is no longer a difficulty within the

very activity of *knowing*. It is but one element of the known. Tragedy and the tragic have been separated.

Reiss 1980: 12

In this case, the tragic idea responds to the Anaximandrian demand for justice (Murphy 2001: 46) once it cannot be addressed on the stage, once theatre can no longer function as a civic institution. John Anton has systematically pursued a very similar argument: 'What was initially a literary device and a dramaturgical concept became an ontological and axiological term with fundamental claims to disclosing the nature of life and the world' (Anton 1993: 32). A dramatic art became a technique of existence: tragedy has been taken off the stage and away from the public realm and has been turned into a special 'sense of life'. As Jaspers warned much earlier:

> It is not the task of philosophy to transfer by analogy tragic categories from the limited knowledge of the world to a comprehensive knowledge of all reality, but rather to discover a language in the code-symbols we hear. ... If preserved in its purity, the original vision of the tragic already contains the essence of philosophy: movement, question, open-mindedness, emotion, wonder, truthfulness, lack of illusion. Philosophy refers to tragic knowledge as to what is inexhaustible in original vision and experience. ... But philosophy refuses to cast this control into the fixed rational terms of a 'tragic philosophy of life'.

Jaspers 1969: 103

Lionel Abel (1967: 175-87) insists that the so-called tragic sense is not something that can be urged on anybody or acquired: neither do philosophers like Pascal or Kierkegaard have it nor do tragedians. It exists only in tragedies and can be recognized only in tragedy's performances – the rest is optimism or pessimism. Franco Moretti agrees that the tragic 'does not exist as a possible situation in human history, whether real or imaginary. Only *tragedy* exists – that is, a particular form of *representing* that history: a rigorously asymmetrical structure marked by a constitutive lack' (Moretti 1983: 55). In a complementary way, Sidney Hook (1967) finds that the most heroic

146

stance is living in a world of inescapable tragedy, using creative intel-
ligence in pragmatic approach and with melioristic attitude. Thus a
pluralistic view of the tragic may be more helpful than an exclusive
(historical, moral or aesthetic) one. It is therefore not a question of
whether tragedy is possible under certain conditions.

As this book began by paying tribute to its oldest predecessor, it
is fitting to close by acknowledging its most recent one. If Szondi's
philosophical study represented an epitaph to German Idealism,
Terry Eagleton's political one offers a comprehensive reconstitution
of the modern tragic tradition. *Sweet Violence* seeks to overcome the
bifurcation of tragic joy into political resignation and aesthetic pleasure (Eagleton 2003: 227) by presenting the tragic as a sceptical
faith necessary for the renewal of ethical politics. In this way, it
manifests convincingly the continued, indeed expanded availability
of this idea.

Clearly, the tragic idea is no longer the sun of Idealist philosophy,
the general concept that both uplifts and destroys thought. That
concept, together with its aesthetic impulse, has collapsed.
Nevertheless, a tragic understanding of the world into which humans
continue to institute and govern their communities remains meaningful for at least three reasons. First, over the centuries, the notion
has acquired so many works, criticisms and interventions that it
carries with it a rich creative and analytical tradition that still invites
new approaches. Second, in several languages the term has acquired
such pliability that it can be applied to voyages and consequences,
decisions and romances, pacts and costs, policies and eras, victories
and failures. When it comes to the fateful interplay of value and folly,
the tragic vocabulary has been able to bounce across cultures, faiths
and systems.

Most importantly, the tragic idea that prevailed after Modernism
and World War Two represents what the notion of *theatrum mundi*
meant to Baroque culture across Europe and the Americas – the
philosophical modality of theatre and theory. In the twenty-first
century, metaphors of the stage once again have come to capture the
worldliness of experience, the transience of life, the weariness of
faith and the melancholy of philosophy. Supreme assurance in knowledge and power, craft and conduct, co-exists with imperious
scepticism. The tragic applies not to essence or existence but to the

dramatic tension that permeates the theatre of the world. What is the place of liberty in it? Are humans actors or viewers, active or passive, real or imagined? As matters of freedom and necessity, autonomy and authority confront us individually and collectively, we sense that tragic responsibility beckons.

Bibliography

Abel, L. (1963), *Metatheatre: A New View of Dramatic Form* (Hill and Wang).
—— (ed.) (1967), *Moderns on Tragedy: An Anthology of Modern and Relevant Opinions on the Substance and Meaning of Tragedy* (Fawcett Publications).
Adler, J. (1983), '"Introduction" to Friedrich Hölderlin, On Tragedy', *Comparative Criticism* 5, 205-30.
Adorno, T.W. ([1933], 1989), *Kierkegaard: Construction of the Aesthetic*, trans. R. Hullot-Kentor (University of Minnesota Press).
Anton, J.P. (1993), 'Nietzsche's Critique of Aristotle's Theory of Tragic Emotions', in N. Georgopoulos (ed.), *Tragedy and Philosophy* (St. Martin's Press).
Arnott, W.G. (1984), 'Nietzsche's View of Greek Tragedy', *Arethusa* 17: 2, 135-49.
Aron, R. (1965), 'Culture and Life' [1938], in L.A. Coser (ed.), *Georg Simmel* (Prentice-Hall).
Auden, W.H. (1967), 'The Christian Tragic Hero' [1945], in Abel (1967).
Augustine (1963), *The Confessions*, trans. R. Warner (New American Library).
Barker, H. (1993), *Arguments for a Theatre* (Manchester University Press).
Batnitzky, L. (2000), *Idolatry and Representation: The Philosophy of Franz Rosenzweig Reconsidered* (Princeton University Press).
Beistegui, M. de (2000), 'Hegel: or The Tragedy of Thinking', in M. de Beistegui and S. Sparks (eds), *Philosophy and Tragedy* (Routledge).
Benjamin, W. ([1928] 1977), *The Origin of Tragic Drama*, trans. J. Osborne (New Left Books).
—— (1978), *Reflections: Essays, Aphorisms, Autobiographical Writings*, trans. E. Jephcott (Harcourt Brace Jovanovich).
—— (1996), *Selected Writings: Volume 1, 1913-26*, ed. M. Bullock and M.W. Jennings (Harvard University Press).
Bennett, B. (1979), *Modern Drama and German Classicism: Renaissance from Lessing to Brecht* (Cornell University Press).
Berdyaev, N. ([1931], 1960), *The Destiny of Man*, trans. N. Duddington (Harper Torchbooks).
Berghahn, K.L. (1992), 'Gedankenfreiheit: From Political Reform to Aesthetic Revolution in Schiller's Works', in E. Bahr and T.P. Saine (eds), *The Internalized Revolution: German Reactions to the French Revolution, 1789-1989* (Garland Press).
Bernstein, J.M. (ed.) (2003), *Classic and Romantic German Aesthetics* (Cambridge University Press).
Bloch, E. (1988), 'The Stage Regarded as a Paradigmatic Institution and the Decision Within It' [1959], in *The Utopian Function of Art and*

Literature: Selected Essays, trans. J. Zipes and F. Mecklenburg (The MIT Press).

———— ([1918], 2000), *The Spirit of Utopia*, trans. A.A. Nassar (Stanford University Press).

Bouchard, L.D. (2001), 'On Contingency and Culpability: Is the Postmodern Post-Tragic?', in J.L. Geddes (ed.), *Evil After Postmodernism: Histories, Narratives, and Ethics* (Routledge).

Brandt, G.W. (ed.) (1998), *Modern Theories of Drama: A Selection of Writings on Drama and Theatre, 1840-1990* (Clarendon Press).

Bretall, R. (ed.) (1973), *A Kierkegaard Anthology* (Princeton University Press).

Burke, J. (2003), *Twin Tracks: The Unexpected Origins of The Modern World* (Simon and Schuster).

Burke, K. (1931), *Counter-Statement* (Harcourt Brace).

———— ([1950], 1969), *A Rhetoric of Motives* (University of California Press).

Carlson, M. ([1984], 1993), *Theories of the Theatre: A Historical and Critical Survey, from the Greeks to the Present* (Cornell University Press).

Cartledge, P. (1997), '"Deep Plays": Theatre as Process in Greek Civic Life', in P.E. Easterling (ed.), *The Cambridge Companion to Greek Tragedy* (Cambridge University Press).

Chytry, J. (1989), *The Aesthetic State: A Quest in Modern German Thought* (University of California Press).

Constant, B. (1983), 'Reflections on Tragedy' [1829], in B.V. Daniels (ed.), *Revolution in the Theatre: French Romantic Theories of Drama* (Greenwood Press).

Courtine, J.-F. ([1988], 1993), 'Tragedy and Sublimity: The Speculative Interpretation of *Oedipus Rex* on the Threshold of German Idealism', in J.-F. Courtine et al., *Of the Sublime: Presence in Question*, trans. J.S. Librett (State University of New York Press).

de Certeau, M. (1986), 'The Freudian Novel: History and Literature' [1981], in *Heterologies: Discourse on the Other*, trans. B. Massumi (University of Minnesota Press).

Deleuze, G. ([1962], 1983), *Nietzsche and Philosophy*, trans. H. Tomlinson (Columbia University Press).

de Quincey, T. (1890), 'Theory of Greek Tragedy', in *The Collected Writings*, New and Enlarged Edition, vol. X: *Literary Theory and Criticism* (Adam and Charles Black).

Dukore, B.F. (ed.) (1974), *Dramatic Theory and Criticism: Greeks to Grotowski* (Harcourt Brace Jovanovich).

Dürrenmatt, F. (1976), *Writings on Theatre and Drama*, trans. H.M. Waidson (Jonathan Cape).

Eagleton, T. (2003), *Sweet Violence: The Idea of the Tragic* (Blackwell).

Erasmo, M. (2004), *Roman Tragedy: Theatre to Theatricality* (University of Texas Press).

Faas, E. (1984), *Tragedy and After: Euripides, Shakespeare, Goethe* (McGill-Queen's University Press).

Ferris, D. (2000), *Silent Urns: Romanticism, Hellenism, Modernity* (Stanford University Press).

Fichte, J.G. (1982), *Science of Knowledge*, trans. P. Hath and J. Lachs (Cambridge University Press).

———— (1992), *Foundations of Transcendental Philosophy: (Wissenschaftslehre) nova methodo (1796/99)*, trans. D. Breazeale (Cornell University Press).

Fiedler, L.A. (1952), Response to 'Our Country and Our Culture: A Symposium', *Partisan Review* 19:3, 294-8.

Freud, S. (1953), *The Interpretation of Dreams* [1900], first part, in *The Standard Edition of the Complete Psychological Works*, vol. IV, trans. J. Strachey (The Hogarth Press).

———— (1955), *Totem and Taboo* [1913], in *The Standard Edition of the Complete Psychological Works,* vol. XIII, trans. J. Strachey (The Hogarth Press).

———— (1963), *Introductory Lectures on Psycho-Analysis* [1916-17], third part, in *The Standard Edition of the Complete Psychological Works*, vol. XVI, trans. J. Strachey (The Hogarth Press).

———— (1966), *The Standard Edition of the Complete Psychological Works*, vol. I: *Pre-Psycho-Analytic Publications and Unpublished Drafts*, trans. J. Strachey (The Hogarth Press).

Gerould, D. (ed.) (2000), *Theatre/Theory/Theatre: The Major Critical Texts* (Applause).

Grass, G. (1999), *My Century*, trans. M.H. Heim (Harcourt).

Guyer, P. (1993), *Kant and the Experience of Freedom: Essays on Aesthetics and Morality* (Cambridge University Press).

Hall, E., F. Macintosh and A. Wrigley (eds) (2004), *Dionysus Since 69: Greek Tragedy at the Dawn of the Third Millennium* (Oxford University Press).

Halliwell, S. (1998), *Aristotle's Poetics* [1986] (University of Chicago Press).

Hebbel, F. ([1844], 1998), Preface to *Mary Magdalene*, excerpted in Brandt (1998).

Hegel, G.W.F. (1948), *Early Theological Writings*, trans. T.M. Knox (University of Pennsylvania Press).

Heidegger, M. ([1953], 1959), *An Introduction to Metaphysics*, trans. R. Manheim (Yale University Press).

———— (1975), 'The Anaximander Fragment' [1950], trans. D.F. Krell, in *Early Greek Thinking* (Harper & Row).

———— (1981), 'Tragedy, Satyr-Play, and Telling Silence in Nietzsche's Thought of Eternal Recurrence', trans. D.F. Krell, *boundary 2* 9:3/10:1, 25-39.

———— ([1982], 2002), *The Essence of Human Freedom: An Introduction to Philosophy*, trans. T. Sadler (Continuum).

Heller, A. and F. Fehér (1991), *The Grandeur and Twilight of Radical Universalism* (Transaction).

Henrich, D. (1997), 'Hegel and Hölderlin' [1971], trans. T. Carman, in *The Course of Remembrance and Other Essays on Hölderlin* (Stanford University Press).

Hölderlin, F. (1988), *Essays and Letters on Theory*, trans. T. Pfau (State University of New York Press).

Hook, S. (1967), 'Pragmatism and the Tragic Sense of Life' [1960], in Abel (1967).

Hugo, V. ([1827], 2000), Preface to *Cromwell*, excerpted in Gerould (2000).

Hume, D. ([1757], 1974), 'Of Tragedy', excerpted in Dukore (1974).

Huxley, A. (1980), 'Tragedy and the Whole Truth' [1931], in R.P. Draper (ed.), *Tragedy: Developments in Criticism* (Macmillan).

Hyman, S.E. (1956), 'Freud and the Climate of Tragedy', *Partisan Review* 23: 2, 198-214.

Ivanov, V. (1960), *Freedom and the Tragic Life: A Study in Dostoevsky,* trans. N. Cameron (The Nonday Press).

—— (1981), 'The Essence of Tragedy' [1912], in L. Senelick (ed. & trans.), *Russian Dramatic Theory from Pushkin to the Symbolists: An Anthology* (University of Texas Press).

—— (1986), 'The Need for Dionysian Theatre' [1906], in M. Green (ed.), *The Russian Symbolist Theatre: An Anthology of Plays and Critical Texts* (Ardis).

Jaspers, K. ([1947], 1969), *Tragedy Is Not Enough*, trans. H.A.T. Reiche, H.T. Moore, and K.W. Deutsch (Archon Books).

Javitch, D. (1999), 'The Assimilation of Aristotle's *Poetics* in Sixteenth-Century Italy', in Norton (1999).

Kant, I. ([1785], 1964), *Groundwork of the Metaphysic of Morals*, trans. H.J. Paton (Harper & Row).

—— ([1928], 1978), *The Critique of Judgement* [1790], trans. J.C. Meredith (Clarendon Press).

Kierkegaard, S. ([1843], 1959), *Either/Or*, trans. D.F. Swenson and L.M. Swenson (Princeton University Press).

—— ([1841], 1965), *The Concept of Irony, with Constant Reference to Socrates*, trans. L.M. Capel (Harper & Row).

Klapp, O.E. (1958), 'Tragedy and the American Climate of Opinion', *Centennial Review of Arts and Sciences* 2, 396-413.

Kolnai, A. (1938), *The War against the West* (Victor Gollancz).

Kracauer, S. ([1963], 1995), 'On the Writings of Walter Benjamin' [1928], in *The Mass Ornament: Weimar Essays*, trans. T.Y. Levin (Harvard University Press).

Krutch, J.W. (1929), *The Modern Temper: A Study and a Confession* (Harcourt, Brace and Company).

Kurzweil, B. (1966), 'Is There such a Thing as Biblical Tragedy?', trans. M.Z. Frank, in I. Cohen and B.Y. Michaoi (eds), *An Anthology of Hebrew Essays*, vol. I (Institute for the Translation of Hebrew Literature).

Lacoue-Labarthe, P. (1978), 'The Caesura of the Speculative', *Glyph* 4, 57-84.

—— (1993), 'The Scene is Primal' [1974], trans. K. McPherson, in *The Subject of Philosophy* (University of Minnesota Press).

Lacoue-Labarthe, P., and J.-L. Nancy (1997), *Retreating the Political*, trans. S. Sparks (Routledge).

Lambropoulos, V. (1993), *The Rise of Eurocentrism: Anatomy of Interpretation* (Princeton University Press).

Langiulli, N. (ed.) (1971), *The Existentialist Tradition: Selected Writings* (Anchor Books).

Lenson, D. (1975), *Achilles' Choice: Examples of Modern Tragedy* (Princeton University Press).

Lessing, G.E. ([1767-9], 1974), *Hamburg Dramatory*, excerpted in Dukore (1974).

Löwy, M. (1991-2), 'Goldmann and Lukács: The Tragic Worldview', *The Philosophical Forum* 23: 1-2, 124-39.

Lukács, G. ([1916], 1971), *The Theory of the Novel*, trans. A. Bostock (The MIT Press).

―――― (1974), 'The Metaphysics of Tragedy' [1911], in *Soul and Form*, trans. A. Bostock (The MIT Press).

Maeterlinck, M. ([1896], 2000), 'The Tragic in Daily Life', in Gerould (2000).

Mann, T. (1958), 'On Schiller' [1955], trans. R. & C. Winston, in *Last Essays*, trans. R. & C. Winston and T. & J. Stern (Alfred A. Knopf).

―――― (1947], 1968), *Doctor Faustus*, trans. H.T. Lowe-Porter (Penguin Books).

Marcuse, H. (1955), *Eros and Civilization: A Philosophical Inquiry into Freud* (Beacon Press).

McDonald, M. and J.M. Walton (eds) (2002), *Amid our Troubles: Irish Versions of Greek Tragedy* (Methuen).

Michel, L. (1956), 'The Possibility of a Christian Tragedy', *Thought*, 403-28.

Moretti, F. (1983), *Signs Taken for Wonders: Essays in the Sociology of Literary Forms*, trans. S. Fischer, D. Forgacs, and D. Miller (NLB).

―――― (1994), 'Modern European Literature: A Geographical Sketch', *New Left Review* 206, 86-109.

Most, G.W. (2000), 'Generating Genres: The Idea of the Tragic', in M. Depew and D. Obbink (eds), *Matrices of Genre: Authors, Canons, and Society* (Harvard University Press).

Mullern, F. (2000), *Culture/Metaculture* (Routledge).

Murdoch, I. (1993), *Metaphysics as a Guide to Morals* (Penguin Press).

Murphy, P. (2001), *Civic Justice: From Greek Antiquity to the Modern World* (Humanity Books).

Nägele, R. (1991), 'The Eyes of the Skull: Benjamin's Aesthetics' [1990], in *Theater, Theory, Speculation: Walter Benjamin and the Scenes of Modernity* (Johns Hopkins University Press).

Nehamas, A. (1985), *Nietzsche: Life as Literature* (Harvard University Press).

Niebuhr, R. (1938), *Beyond Tragedy: Essays on the Christian Interpretation of History* (C. Scribner's Sons).

Nietzsche, F. (1967), *The Birth of Tragedy and The Case of Wagner*, trans. W. Kaufmann (Vintage Books).

―――― (1979), *Philosophy and Truth: Selections from Nietzsche's Notebooks of the Early 1870s*, trans. D. Breazeale (Humanities Press International).

―――― (2003), *Writings from the Late Notebooks*, trans. K. Sturge (Cambridge University Press).

Norton, G.P. (ed.) (1999), *The Cambridge History of Literary Criticism. Volume 3: The Renaissance* (Cambridge University Press).

Novalis (1997), *Philosophical Writings*, trans. M. Stoljar (State University of New York Press).

Nussbaum, M.C. (1991), 'The Transfigurations of Intoxication: Nietzsche, Schopenhauer, and Dionysus', *Arion* (3rd Series) 1:2, 75-111.

Patsalidis, S. and E. Sakellaridou (eds) (1999), *(Dis)Placing Classical Greek Theatre* (University Studio Press).

Pinkard, T. (2002), *German Philosophy 1760-1860: The Legacy of Idealism* (Cambridge University Press).

Pippin, R.B. (1997), *Idealism as Modernism: Hegelian Variations* (Cambridge University Press).

Porter, J.I. (2000), *Nietzsche and the Philology of the Future* (Stanford University Press).

Prawer, S.S. (1976), *Karl Marx and World Literature* (Clarendon Press).

Rapin, R. ([1674], 1974), *Reflections on Aristotle's Treatise of Poesy*, excerpted in Dukore (1974).

Rehm, R. (2003), *Radical Theatre: Greek Tragedy and the Modern World* (Duckworth).

Reiss, T.J. (1980), *Tragedy and Truth: Studies in the Development of a Renaissance and Neoclassical Discourse* (Yale University Press).

——— (1999), 'Renaissance Theatre and the Theory of Tragedy', in Norton (1999).

——— (2002), *Against Autonomy: Global Dialectics of Cultural Exchange* (Stanford University Press).

Richards, J.H. (1991), *Theater Enough: American Culture and the Metaphor of the World Stage, 1607-1789* (Duke University Press).

Rocco, C. (1996), *Tragedy and Enlightenment: Athenian Political Thought and the Dilemmas of Modernity* (University of California Press).

Rosenzweig, F. ([1921], 1971), *The Star of Redemption*, trans. W.W. Hallo (Holt, Rinehart and Winston).

Ruprecht, Jr, L.A. (1994), *Tragic Posture and Tragic Vision: Against the Modern Failure of Nerve* (Continuum).

Saint-Évremond, C. de M. de ([1672], 1974), 'On Ancient and Modern Tragedy', in Dukore (1974).

Santayana, G. (1936), 'Tragic Philosophy', *Scrutiny* 4: 4, 365-76.

Sartre, J.-P. (1976), 'Forgers of Myths' [1946], in *Sartre on Theater*, trans. F. Jellinek (Pantheon Books).

Scheler, M. (1965), 'On the Tragic' [1915], trans. B. Stambler, in R.W. Corrigan (ed.), *Tragedy: Vision and Form* (Chandler).

Schelling, F.W.J. (1980), *The Unconditional in Human Knowledge: Four Early Essays (1794-1796)*, trans. F. Marti (Bucknell University Press).

——— ([1859], 1989), *The Philosophy of Art*, trans. D.W. Stott (University of Minnesota Press).

Schiller, F. (1902), *Aesthetical and Philosophical Essays* (P.F. Collier & Son).

——— (1959), 'The Stage Considered as a Moral Institution' [1785], trans. J.B. Greene, in *An Anthology for Our Time* (Frederick Ungar).

——— (2003), 'Kallias or Concerning Beauty: Letters to Gottfried Körner' [1793], trans. S. Bird-Pollan, in Bernstein (2003).

Schlegel, A. ([1809-11], 1974), *Lectures on Dramatic Art and Literature*, excerpted in Dukore (1974).

Schmidt, D.J. (2001), *On Germans and Other Greeks: Tragedy and the Ethical Life* (Indiana University Press).

Schneewind, J.B. (1998), *The Invention of Autonomy: A History of Modern Moral Philosophy* (Cambridge University Press).

Schopenhauer, A. ([1818], 1974), *The World as Will and Idea*, excerpted in Dukore (1974).

Schulte-Sasse, J. (ed.) (1997), *Theory as Practice: A Critical Anthology of Early German Romantic Writings* (University of Minnesota Press).

—— (1988), 'The Concept of Literary Criticism in German Romanticism, 1795-1810', in P.U. Hohendahl (ed.), *A History of German Literary Criticism, 1730-1980* (University of Nebraska Press).

—— (ed.) (1997), *Theory as Practice: A Critical Anthology of Early German Romantic Writings* (University of Minnesota Press).

Scott, C.E. (1996), *On the Advantages and Disadvantages of Ethics and Politics* (Indiana University Press).

Shelley, P.B. (1909), *Literary and Philosophical Criticism*, ed. J. Shawcross (H. Frowde).

Shestov, L. ([1937], 1966), *Athens and Jerusalem*, trans. B. Martin (Ohio University Press).

Silk, M.S. (ed.) (1996), *Tragedy and the Tragic: Greek Theatre and Beyond* (Oxford University Press).

Silk, M.S. and J.P. Stern (1980), *Nietzsche on Tragedy* (Cambridge University Press).

Simmel, G. (1968), 'On the Concept and the Tragedy of Culture' [1911], in *The Conflict in Modern Culture and Other Essays*, trans. K.P. Etzkorn (Teachers College Press).

Simon, B. (1988), *Tragic Drama and the Family: Psychoanalytic Studies from Aeschylus to Beckett* (Yale University Press).

Sologub, F. (1986), 'The Theater of One Will' [1908], in R.F. Peterson (ed.), *The Russian Symbolists: An Anthology of Critical and Theoretical Writings* (Ardis).

Soni, V. (forthcoming), 'Trials and Tragedies: The Literature of Unhappiness'.

Sontag, S. (1966), 'The Death of Tragedy' [1963], in *Against Interpretation and Other Essays* (Farrar, Straus & Giroux).

Spengler, O. ([1918], 1926), *The Decline of the West. Vol. I: Form and Actuality*, trans. C.F. Atkinson (Alfred A. Knopf).

Starr, P. (1995), *Logics of Failed Revolt: French Theory after May '68* (Stanford University Press).

Steiner, G. ([1961], 1963), *The Death of Tragedy* (Faber and Faber).

—— (1984), *Antigones* (Clarendon Press).

Struve, W. (1973), *Elites against Democracy: Leadership Ideals in Bourgeois Political Thought in Germany, 1890-1933* (Princeton University Press).

Szondi, P. ([1961], 2002), *An Essay on the Tragic*, trans. P. Fleming (Stanford University Press).

Taminiaux, J. (1993), *Poetics, Speculation, and Judgment: The Shadow of the Work of Art from Kant to Phenomenology*, trans. M. Gendre (State University of New York Press).

Taxidou, O. (2004), *Tragedy, Modernity and Mourning* (Edinburgh University Press).

Tucker, R.C. (ed.) (1978), *The Marx-Engels Reader* (W.W. Norton).

Unamuno, M. de ([1913], 1954), *The Tragic Sense of Life*, trans. J.E. Crawford Flitch (Dover).

Wagner, R. (1966), *Prose Works*, vol. 8, trans. W.A. Ellis (Broude Bros.).

—— (1995), *Prose Works*, vol. 2, trans. W.A. Ellis (University of Nebraska Press).

Warminski, A. (1987), *Readings in Interpretation: Hölderlin, Hegel, Heidegger* (University of Minnesota Press).

Wellbery, D.E. (ed.) (2004), *A New History of German Literature* (Harvard University Press).

Wetmore, Jr, K.J. (2002), *The Athenian Sun in an African Sky: Modern African Adaptations of Classical Greek Tragedy* (McFarland & Company).

White, H. (1973), *Metahistory: The Historical Imagination in Nineteenth-Century Europe* (Johns Hopkins University Press).

Williams, B. (1993), *Shame and Necessity*, Sather Classical Lectures, Vol. 57 (University of California Press).

Wolin, R. (1980), 'An Aesthetics of Redemption: Benjamin's Path to *Trauerspiel*', *Telos* 43, Spring, 61-90.

Žižek, S. (2001), *Did Somebody Say Totalitarianism? Five Interventions in the (Mis)use of a Notion* (Verso).

Index of Names